KAREN LEARY

She Pees Like a Horse!

Confessions of a School Principal

Acknowledgements

To my husband, **Scott Leary**, thank you for holding my hand and walking our shared career path ahead of me, for making me laugh every single day, for challenging me intellectually, and for loving me so sweetly and completely.

To my daughter, **Jennifer Holloway**, thank you for those countless childhood evenings you spent in my classrooms, for making me laugh, and for always, in every way, making me proud.

To **Michael Miles Miller**, thank you for your encouraging words and for the gift of editing mine.

To the thousands of students and hundreds of educators during my career, thank you for teaching me!

Dedication

For Mary Roselli—here's to you, Mary Lou!

Table of Contents

"What do you want to be when you grow up?" I asked the petite and ponytailed kindergartner. "I want to be a teacher," she said, smiling up at me, "or else a beautiful mermaid princess."

CHAPTER ONE

"Come Back When You Grow Up, Girl"

S HE PEES LIKE A HORSE!

It was a Tuesday, so we were gathered together for one of our principals meetings, from which we were taking a ten-minute break.

As if the loud, strong and steady stream weren't enough of a clue as to the youthfulness of the woman occupying the restroom stall adjoining mine, I could also see the sharply pointed toes of her red high heels peeking out from under the puddle of black pant legs encircling her ankles.

I used to wear shoes like that, I thought—looking down at my black suede Cole Haan flats—round-toed, with their cushioned Nike soles and custom orthopedic insoles tucked inside.

I used to pee like that, too.

In a hunched-over tripod—elbows pressing uncomfortably into my thighs—I laced my fingers together and patiently waited. Getting pretty close to needing a manicure, I noticed, pushing each nail's cuticle downward with the tip of my thumbnail.

Always one to take advantage of an opportunity to multitask, I lifted my Kate Spade from the fold-down metal shelf and placed it on my lap. From inside the purse, I fished out three Dentyne gum wrappers (one with a petrified wad inside), the previous Sunday's church bulletin, a half-eaten Kit Kat candy bar, an old grocery list, and four Starbucks receipts. I tucked the Kit Kat back inside the zippered pocket (it wasn't that old) and crumpled the other items before dropping them inside the white metal box affixed to the stall.

Last dribble-dribble dropped just in time. From outside the restroom's door I heard a muffled voice over the microphone asking everyone to please return to their seat. The "horse," of course, left the ladies room quite a while ago—her high heels clickity-clacking across the tile floor as she hurriedly scurried toward the door. I imagined her already seated, Starbucks venti macchiato on the table in front of her, pen in hand, bright-eyed, and raring to go.

I always had a love-hate relationship with Tuesday meetings. Much as I welcomed any opportunity to see colleagues, I'd rather have been back in my school. Principals pay dearly for time away from their schools—returning to blinking phone message lights, unopened emails, discipline referrals, letters and forms to sign, and two or three students waiting to "see" the principal. On Tuesdays, playing catch-up always consumed the balance of the school day.

As a child I absolutely loved school. School was my happy place and my safe haven. Unlike at home, at school no one ever yelled or cursed at me. No one ever scared me or hit me. I loved school and school loved me back.

Back then, I didn't realize I was what educators sometimes refer to as an "at-risk" student—one who's frequently absent and slipping behind academically. I didn't have a clue until years later when, as an adult, I ran across my old diary from the third grade. The small and badly scuffed pink book was locked and its tiny gold key long gone. With scissors, I snipped the thin leatherette strap stretching across the gilt-edged pages. There it was—indisputable evidence of my "at risk" status written across the pages in my own childhood scrawls.

First few days in January I'd faithfully recorded entries with a dull pencil in messy cursive. By mid-February, entries became a little hit-and-miss, and, by the end of March, the balance of the diary's pages had been left completely blank.

January 5 *Had to go to the bored for arithmitic races so I pertended to drop the chawk. Ha!*

January 6 *Had to stay home from school today and clean the whole house for mommie.*

January 7 *Mommie made me stay home to do grocery shoping. This list was SO long. It took me along time to get everthing. Hope I get to go to school tommorrow.*

February 5 *It's my birthday today but when I got home from school mommie said it won't be my birthday today. I am sad and mad at her.*

February 8 *It is not my birthday. I got a D on the spelling test. I hat spelling! Lisa and I played hop scoch at recess. It was fun. Maryanne was sick today.*

February 9 *Went on a feeld trip to the bread bakry. It was so fun. They gave us all a loof of bread. I hided it in my room. Ricky got spanked for going to his friends house after school. Not my birthday agin. Oh well.*

I missed a lot of elementary school. My mother—manic some days, depressed most—sometimes kept me home to do housework and, other times, just to keep her company. Consequently, I also missed a lot of learning. Thankfully, the time and effort some exceptional teachers put into my academic growth paid off. When I was old enough to make my own choices I never missed school and, whenever anyone would ask me what I wanted to become when I grew up, not too surprisingly, my answer was always "a teacher."

After high school I joined the U. S. Navy. It was an atypical choice for a young girl but, I had a plan. During the Vietnam war, enlistees were entitled (upon honorable discharge) to access the GI Bill to pay for college tuition. Being in the Navy was a wonderful experience. I finished my three-year tour and started college immediately after discharge.

The subsequent birth of my daughter was a delightful detour and I was fortunate to be a stay-at-home mom during her childhood. Twelve years later I picked up where I left off. I finished earning my bachelor's degree and became a first-grade teacher in the same school where I student taught.

In my second year I switched to fourth grade and decided to pursue a master's in administration to obtain principal credentials, just to have options.

After only six years of teaching, that option became available to me—landing in my lap in a most unconventional way. I was a fifth-grade teacher, attending an educator's conference with the principal and six other teachers from our school. During one of the conference sessions, after we'd all finished reading and discussing assigned chapters from the presenter's new book, each table group was being asked to choose a representative to share their learning with the roomful of conference attendees.

The principal said, "Ms. Leary, y'all are good at this kind of thing. Go for it! Just keep in mind, how well you do on this presentation will determine whether or not you get the assistant principal's job."

He was laughing, but I strongly suspected he wasn't kidding. His current assistant principal had been selected for another district position for the upcoming school year and I'd already mentioned to the principal I was interested in applying for her job.

So, when it was our table's turn, I stood up, fluffed my hair, pushed up the sleeves of my pink sweater, and looked out at the faces of a hundred plus fellow educators.

"Okay, y'all, listen up," I called out with a big smile, "because, I really do need everybody's help right now."

"Our principal just said that my getting the assistant principal's job at our school next year all rides on how well I do with this presentation," I explained.

"So, would y'all be kind enough to 'ooh' and 'ahh' after everything I say? Clap extra loud at the end. Oh, and if y'all are feeling especially kind, a standing ovation would be a real nice touch!"

After that shameless self-promoting introduction, I briefly explained what the chapter was about and shared our group's take on what it all meant. The "oohs and ahhs" were plentiful, the clapping robust, and they did, in fact, join in a standing ovation. A couple of sweet ladies at a nearby table yelled, "Encore!" and a man near the back made one of those loud two-fingers-in-the-mouth kind of whistles.

The principal said something about me being dangerous and that I should probably have his job. I was riding high for the next couple days and very excited about next year's promotion.

That Saturday—the day after returning from the conference—I got a phone call from the principal. Almost immediately I could tell by his tone he felt horrible about what he was about to tell me. Two other staff members heard what happened during the conference. Turns out, they both were interested in and qualified for the assistant principal position; so, to be fair, the principal decided he had to conduct formal interviews.

Wearing my best dark blue skirted suit, with a single strand of pearls, I answered all of the questions to the best of my ability. I was chosen for the job and will be forever grateful for that opportunity to serve as his assistant principal for one year. During that year, the principal was promoted to regional superintendent and was away from the building a great deal. Consequently, a lot of end-of-year closure responsibilities fell upon me. This man was the best mentor I could have ever asked for and that year was the best training ground I could have ever experienced. By year's end, I felt completely confident I was ready to take on the leadership responsibilities of having my own school.

As a first-year principal (back when I, too, peed like a horse) I was going to change the world or, at least, my school. And, why not? I was young, well trained, and had all the answers (or so I thought). I was going to be the beloved, cool school principal. I was going to lead my teachers to become the best they could be, and our students would be super achievers. I was going to create a learning and work environment that was exciting and fun to be a part of and, I would do it all while wearing red high heels.

Somewhere along the line I became slightly disillusioned from exposure to reality and, at some point, I donated my favorite pair of red high heels to the local Salvation Army.

I tossed the damp paper towel into the restroom's trash container and retrieved the tube of Chanel lipstick from my purse and quickly reapplied a thin layer of Rouge Allure. In the mirror I caught the reflection of my photo ID badge dangling at the end of the lanyard around my neck. In that much younger photo, my thick hair was dark brown and hung well past my shoulders. The day the photo was taken, I was wearing fuchsia-pink lipstick and a black and pink argyle-patterned sweater—a very 1980's look—although the photo was taken in the early nineties.

Looking at the photo made me recall a time when I was monitoring the cafeteria during the first-grade lunch period. A curly-haired girl ran up to me and threw her arms around my waist. Oh, how I loved those unsolicited expressions of affection, although they made for some pretty hefty monthly dry-cleaning bills.

The little cutie reached up and took hold of my ID badge. She studied it for a moment and then looked up at me and then back down at the card. In the sweetest voice she proclaimed, "Mrs. Leary, you look lots prettier in your picture than you do in your real life." In my defense, at that time, the picture was some fifteen years, three hair colors, and twenty-five pounds outdated.

Funny how time moves so very quickly yet, we're barely aware of its passing. It's like you just keep reporting for duty over and over and over and then, one day, you sit down to get something out of the back of a bottom cabinet and getting up from off of the floor takes a whole lot more effort than it ever did before and you realize—Damn, I'm old—when did THIS happen?

Back in the meeting room, only about half of the principals were seated, allowing enough time for a stop at the coffee setup to get a cup of too-strong coffee made tolerable by that white powdered cream substitute stuff and a packet of raw sugar.

According to the printed meeting agenda the balance of the morning would be spent covering the usual early spring topics: state testing, safety drills, teacher evaluations, custodial duties, and such. Most of it routine for all but the district's most inexperienced principals.

One of the benefits of becoming a ranking member of the principals' cadre was that less experienced principals called upon us for suggestions and advice. They figured by now we veterans had probably encountered about every problem and crisis and just might have the answers they needed. Sometimes we did. Sometimes we didn't. But I do know it felt gratifying just to be called upon.

The circumstances surrounding obtaining my second administrative job were a bit unusual as well. My husband and I had flown across the country so he could interview for an administrative position. After the interview he told me we should stop at a district south of where we were because he knew the superintendent; and, since we weren't going to fly back home for a couple more days, we had time for a road trip.

Several years prior, my husband had taken an undergraduate class from this superintendent (back in the days when he was a professor at one of the state colleges). We mentioned this to the superintendent's secretary when asking if he might have a few minutes for us just to say hello. We were soon led into his office, where he greeted my husband like a long-lost friend.

"Well, how are you, Scott?" he said extending his hand. "Good to see you, man. Been a long time!"

After a little bit of small talk, the superintendent said, "Hey, if I remember right, weren't you one hell of a tennis player when you were in college?"

My husband just laughed politely and said a single word, "Well…," which trailed off ending with a smile, a nod, and a shrug.

Don't get me wrong, my husband has many skills and talents; tennis however, is not among them. For the balance of the meeting, we were certain the superintendent was pretending he remembered my husband as a college student. Not that my husband ever expected that he would have been remembered. But it worked out well, because while he pretended, we just pretended not to know he was pretending.

When he asked what brought us to the area, Scott told him he was interviewing. The superintendent picked up the phone and asked his secretary to ask a director to join us. She entered the room within minutes. The director was a tiny woman who smelled faintly of cigarettes and perfume. She wore huge square-rimmed glasses and lots of yellow-gold jewelry. Her manner was friendly although somewhat abrupt. She asked us a handful of questions and then left the room to make a couple of phone calls. She returned to let us know she had lined up a school tour for us that afternoon and interviews the following morning.

About a month later, we got an evening phone call from a gentleman introducing himself as the director of human resources. He said he really hoped we were still interested in administrative positions because our being hired was just announced during the school board meeting.

"Hey, buddy, you're late!" the counselor said to the student who entered the office ten minutes after the tardy bell. The second-grade boy responded, "I can't be late. I just got here."

CHAPTER TWO

"Just Call Out My Name"

I WAS AN ELEMENTARY SCHOOL PRINCIPAL FOR SEVENTEEN years. During his career, my husband was an administrator of both elementary and middle schools for a total of twenty-six years. Our daughter (who at an early age swore she'd never work in a school) became a school psychologist and has worked at both high school and elementary levels.

Our careers in public education made for a wealth of stories—ranging from humorous to horrific—which we sometimes shared during family gatherings and holiday dinners (with all confidential, identifying personal information and names withheld, of course).

Regarding names, this also meant that both times our daughter and son-in-law were expecting a child, we provided them a do-not-name-the-baby-this list. Thanks to nose pickers, whiners, screamers, hitters and spitters, a number of names had to be off limits—a consequence of the profession. Couldn't be Max, Jayden, Raven, or Cooper. No Stephanie, Jocelyn, Ariel, or Dahlia and, for God's sake, not Aiden!

When I was a child growing up in California, I remember names being pretty straightforward and unimaginative. You know—Debbie,

Billy, Susie, Bobby. Back then the names list was so short that in any classroom there was bound to be more than one student with the same first name, necessitating the inclusion of last name initials to avoid mixups—Kathy P., Kathy R., Bobby M., Bobby S.

I was the only Karen in my second-grade class until another Karen entered a few days after the start of school. The teacher dubbed her Karen A., and the poor girl continued to be Karen A. for three years after, even though we were never again in the same classroom.

During the course of my career, a lot of names went in and out of popularity. Despite these trends, biblical names always had their place (e.g., Mary, John, Sarah, James, Michael).

In the late eighties, names previously thought of as last names—like Taylor, Jameson, McKenzie, Kramer, and Kennedy—became popular choices for first names.

At one school we had a few little girls named Nevaeh ("heaven" spelled backward). Around that same time, we enrolled several girls bearing idyllic names like Precious, Lovely, Princess, Angel, and even a Heaven Leigh. I don't know, just seemed like a lot of expectation of perfection to place upon a little kid.

For a few years, the trendy names from five or so years prior made our kindergarten rosters look as though they had been filled in by John Denver (Meadow, Sierra, Cricket, Willow, Cedar, Juniper, Aspen). During that period I met a Rainbow, a Sunshine, a Thunder, and a Breezy. One year we enrolled a little boy named Lyon and a little girl named Tiger.

I laughed when our school's office clerk said, "All we need now is a Bear. Oh, my!"

Then, old-fashioned names made their return—those monikers formerly bestowed upon our grandfathers and great aunts: Walter, Hazel, Ida, Otto, Mabel, Violet, Edith and Howard.

By the time I was nearing retirement, I thought I had heard them all. I was wrong. During my final year as a principal, I met a numbered student.

When she was expecting her fourth child, his mother found out she was having another boy. The other three boys' names all began with the same letter. Let's say it was the letter "E." According to his mom, the family couldn't come to an agreement on another name that began with the letter "E" so, they just decided to name the baby E-four. Yep, that's right, E-four. (True story—letter changed to protect his privacy).

During the same school year, the sassiest little redhead ran up to me during morning recess. She reached up and folded her little hand around mine and cheerfully informed me she was "the new kid in school."

"Oh, so, you're the one," I teased. "I have been wanting to meet you."

She giggled, flashing an adorable missing-toothed grin. I told her my name and she told me hers.

"What a pretty name." I said. "I don't think I've ever met anyone named Harley before."

She shared that she was named Harley because she was conceived while her parents were on vacation. They had ridden their Harley to Disneyland. Didn't know quite how to respond to that, so I just asked if she had any brothers or sisters.

"Just my baby brother," she responded. "Ford."

A kindergarten girl sitting motionless on a playground swing began waving at me and called out: "Excuse me, school princess. Can you please push me?"

CHAPTER THREE

"Blackbird"

DURING TUESDAY MEETINGS, WE'RE SEATED AROUND round tables. No one really had an assigned seat and yet, we kind of did. Tuesday after Tuesday, many of us chose to sit in the same chair at the same table with the same people. High school folks usually gravitated toward the front of the room and elementary settled more toward the back. District office personnel always occupied seats on the left-hand side at the very front of the room.

Each Tuesday a mini parade of district office folks distributed stapled packets of handouts and when his or her scheduled time slot arrived, he or she would proceed to read the handouts to us during a PowerPoint presentation.

I always tuned in enough to know what was expected of me and tuned out enough to maintain a positive attitude. On this particular Tuesday, the information being shared was already familiar and I knew where and how to access whatever I needed to complete the tasks. So, I spent a little time daydreaming about a vacation my husband and I had taken a few years back.

Spring break in Paris. Oh, my, how absolutely delightful!

One day, while walking toward the corner café near the Louvre for yet another addictive breakfast of pain au chocolate avec cappuccino, we were passed on the sidewalk by two straight and silent lines of eight or nine-year-old girls who appeared to be on a field trip. Two teachers were leading the lines of *petites filles*. Each child was dressed in the most darling plaid-skirted uniform and crisply ironed white blouse with a neatly-tied black bow beneath her buttoned collar—all of them looking oh so very "Madeline."

I think a principal wears a uniform of sorts. Male elementary principals tend to wear sport coats or sweaters over crisp collared shirts. Their secondary school counterparts tend to dress in a little more "business attire," wearing suits or at least donning ties with their sport coats. Of course, at least in my experience, location was a factor—the southern states being more formal and conservative in dress than the western ones.

In the eighties, when my career began, women teachers wore mostly dresses or skirts. Men wore neatly pressed collared shirts and many wore ties. By the end of my career, dress changed considerably. Now it isn't unusual for both men and women staff members to wear jeans. I worked in six schools. At all of them, Friday was the designated "casual dress" day—even for administrators. Today, it would be hard to tell a casual day from a regular day.

Long ago, I realized that black is my friend. Black best hides fingerprints from kindergartners' hip-level hugs and third-graders' attention-getting shoulder taps. While I was working, on any given day I might attend a district-level training, take the family of a prospective student on a tour of the school, hold back the long hair of a little girl vomiting in the health room, and attend an evening PTA meeting. Might even join the custodian in mopping up a flooding boys' restroom, stand recess duty in the rain, and, of course, open countless sticky juice boxes in the cafeteria. Consequently, stashed in one of my bottom desk drawers was a plastic bag containing a pair of black flats and an extra outfit—just in case.

One cloudy afternoon, during dismissal, I was standing carpool duty with an administrative colleague when a young student, whom neither of us knew by name, approached us.

"Do they make you guys dress alike?" she asked.

We each did a quick glance at the other and started laughing—black blazers over black A-line dresses, worn with black tights, black high heels, and ID badges hanging from lanyards. The only traces of originality were the earrings and watches we'd each chosen to wear.

"No, darling, they don't make us dress alike. But it sure does look that way, doesn't it?"

Today's teacher dresses far more comfortably than I did when I was teaching. My teaching wardrobe consisted of skirted suits, skirts with blouses and cardigans, and dresses—often worn, of course, with my signature red high heels. I liked it that way.

I believe how a teacher dresses sends a message to the kids. Once in a while, one of my students would remark about what I was wearing. I always responded to "You look nice today, Mrs. Leary" with "Thank you. I like to dress up for my students."

I wanted to send the message that they're worth it. I also wanted to send a message to the schools' parent community that I was a professional deserving of respect. That might have been a harder sell had I been wearing a Panther's sweatshirt, shredded blue jeans, and athletic shoes.

Just my opinion.

Although it certainly was not an original idea, I brought a "spirit day" tradition to four of the schools in which I worked. Spirit Day was always on the first Friday of each month. Student leadership club (or student council) was responsible for choosing the theme for each spirit day's dress. I had veto power, of course, in case the chosen theme was inappropriate or controversial—like the time "gender bender" was suggested (when girls would dress as boys and boys would dress as girls). That one had letters to the editor and viral YouTube videos written all over it.

A favorite of kids in all the schools was "crazy hair day," when students and staff donned wigs, curlers, hair accessories, spiked hair, etc. Another was "friends and twins day," when both students and staff would pair up with a friend and dress as alike as possible.

To encourage participation, and as a fun reward for our hard-working employees, I always provided first, second, and third-place costume prizes for staff—usually Starbucks cards I had purchased. Once in a while, when feeling particularly brave, I'd hit the streets asking local businesses for prize donations (movie tickets, free dinners, etc.).

One year, on friends and twins day, an entire grade-level team dressed like Catholic nuns wearing black ankle-length jumpers over white turtlenecks, along with very noticeable large crosses hanging on the end long chains. That one worried me slightly thinking I might end up fielding a few parent phone calls. Not so much because of their costumes, but because they kept chanting and making the sign of the cross over students saying, "Bless you, my child."

Two particular Spirit Day themes really added weight to the theory that how we dress affects our behavior: pajama day and dress for success.

Pajama day was usually scheduled on the first Friday in December. Those cozy flannels, furry slippers, and plush robes kept everyone a bit calmer and quieter throughout the day—staff and students alike.

The same thing happened on "dress for success" day, which, for students, usually meant wearing church clothes or an outfit they might choose for picture day. There were always a number of frilly dresses and little boys wearing the cutest miniature suits with clip-on ties. Misbehaviors dropped significantly and even the most challenging students became uncharacteristically well-mannered. It was uncanny!

The most-deserved first-place prize for "dress for success" once went to the paraprofessional who came to work wearing a graduation cap and gown. She even wore her keepsake tassel and carried her framed diploma. What an ingenious way to model and inspire student success.

One year, my own "dress for success" outfit was a navy-blue St. John suit, worn with a strand of opera-length pearls, and a pair of blue-suede Marc Jacobs high heels. Our associate principal wore a sweatshirt with an embroidered and sequined Christmas picture on it, paired with white pants, and silver-sequined Converse tennis shoes.

Every morning the associate and I walked the halls together peeking inside each classroom. On that day, while "dressed for success," the first student we encountered during our morning rounds excitedly called out to the associate, "Wow! You look SO beautiful!" Happened repeatedly. All. Day. Long. You just can't compete with sequins.

"I need to register my kids," the mother standing at the counter said. "But first I need to know, are you the school that gives away the really great Thanksgiving baskets, and, if you're not, can you tell me which school is?"

CHAPTER FOUR

"Love's Not a Competition (But I'm Winning)"

C OMPETITION IS HEALTHY—TO A POINT. DURING THE Tuesday meetings, if we weren't careful, the line between sharing successes and just plain showing off would begin to blur and become painfully thin. Often a principal would be called upon (in advance) to prepare a presentation for his or her colleagues.

Over time, many of the principals shared with one another (during in-the-parking-lot and off-the-record conversations) that they felt uncomfortable addressing colleagues like they were the expert on whatever topic was presented. Funny how even among a group of principals, all of whom had master's degrees or doctorates, there still existed that middle school kid's fear of not wanting to appear "full of oneself."

In one district in which I worked, Friday's last email from our supervisor would often have an assignment that was to be completed and then shared during the following week's meeting. Might be something as simple as orally sharing what we're doing in our building to reduce student tardiness. Sometimes, however, the assignment would send several of us into a tailspin. We were once asked to analyze our school's student progress (at three grade levels) on a particular reading assessment (over a three-year period) and to create a graphic depiction of the trends we were seeing. Sounds pretty straightforward now, but, this was then— back in the earlier days of technology. We'd pretty much mastered using computers for email and word processing. Most of us weren't yet tech savvy when it came to publishing, graphics, and such. Admittedly, some of us would have been far more at home playing *Oregon Trail* than creating an Excel spreadsheet. (Always choose to be the banker, by the way.)

That following Tuesday, each principal took his or her turn at the big white screen in front of the roomful of colleagues. Several bar graphs and line graphs were shown. There was even a pie graph thrown in the mix, although that choice didn't seem to make much sense.

Some of us admitted to one another that we'd sought the help of a teacher who was good with computers or a computer lab para-educator. One principal enlisted the help of a neighbor who worked at the Apple store at the mall.

Each graph was looking better than the one before—more colorful, larger, easier to understand. One person even embedded graphs in a PowerPoint. There's an over-achiever in every crowd.

Thankfully, one of our colleagues took his place in the show-and-tell spotlight, and instantly halted what was again inching its way toward becoming a culture of unhealthy competition. Opening a plain manila folder, he took out a single sheet of white copier paper on which he had drawn a not-too-perfect bar graph using nothing more than a rather dull No. 2 pencil. The silence in the room was quickly replaced with hearty laughter.

And, we're back!

A first-grade boy sitting next to me was staring at my face. He pointed to a small flat mole above my upper lip and asked, "What's that?" I explained it was just a mole and that some people actually call them beauty marks. With furrowed brow and narrowed eyes he stared at it for a few more seconds and then asked me, "Do you wish you didn't have it?"

CHAPTER FIVE

"Harper Valley P.T.A."

ALTHOUGH THERE WERE SIMILARITIES IN EACH OF the principals jobs I held, the jobs were by no means the same. A couple of schools had 700+ students and nearly 100 staff members. Others had half as many students and staff. Daily duties and challenges varied as much as school sizes.

In one community I was an administrator in a communications magnet school. It was a huge, beautiful building housing a state-of-the-art technology lab and its own television studio. Although it was a public school, a large portion of the students were selected via a lottery system. About twenty percent of the students resided in the school's lovely planned community, and, for the most part, the families were very financially healthy.

Our track wasn't paved. Parents of one of our students thought it would be nicer for children to run on asphalt, so they gifted the entire cost of the project to the school. Cars pulling up at dismissal always included a number of newer BMWs, Mercedes, and Jaguars. Every year the fifth-graders experienced a sightseeing trip to Washington, DC, via luxury-chartered buses and a four-day stay at a very nice hotel.

Our PTA membership was so large that the monthly meetings were held in the auditorium. The biggest issue was to make sure we wouldn't have over $100,000.00 on the books at the end of each school year, because that would cause PTA to lose its *non-profit* designation for income tax purposes.

When another school's PTA board needed to decide how to spend money earmarked for after-school activities, they solicited my input. I suggested a school chorus. We already had a qualified staff member willing to serve as director and we had a growing number of English Language Learners. I shared with the ladies that research suggests a new language is more easily and quickly acquired through singing.

The PTA board ladies exchanged glances with one another. Then, the most outspoken of the group cut to the chase by telling me they'd already decided on tennis lessons. She said we really need to offer something that appeals to our more "typical" students because our school was already changing too much.

"The wrong people are moving into this school," she said with her head tilted and eyes widened. "Do you understand what I'm saying?" she said nodding her head and then pursing her lips a bit.

Yes, unfortunately, I did.

One of my favorite memories from a principals' party we held at our home happened when several of us wandered into my husband's music room. He and a good friend pulled a couple of guitars from their stands and began softly strumming while the rest of us listened and sipped our party drinks.

Without prompting, one of the female principals began singing a perfect rendition of Jeannie C. Riley's 1968 hit, "Harper Valley PTA," after which she received a hearty round of applause.

I loved that she felt comfortable enough to do that. It was an unexpected delight, and she couldn't have chosen a better song for a group of principals than one about a parent teacher association.

PTAs operate differently at every school. The PTA at one K-5 school I worked in resembled a bickering dysfunctional family in a television sitcom. During the first PTA board meeting, the ladies were excitedly telling me all about their recent retreat. When they first began talking, I thought they'd each paid to attend some state or national PTA event. If only!

Using our school's PTA funds, they enjoyed a three-day girls' getaway at the beach. I recall thinking at the time, this can't possibly be a legal use of money raised by students. As a principal, sometimes you just really wish you could unsee or unhear things. Mid-year, this same group of ladies got into quite a feud that ended with them voting the vice president "off the island."

At another school, the mix of parents on the PTA board often made for an unusual mix of discussion topics. Our school housed three classes comprised of students who lived in all different areas of town. The balance of the school population was from the school's primarily lower socioeconomic neighborhood. During one PTA meeting, a man brought up the idea of asking the district to install tall chain length fencing around the perimeter of the school because of the growing problems of transients, drug usage, and crime in the school's neighborhood. Soon afterward, a woman excitedly floated the idea of holding a PTA-sponsored ski equipment swap. Two different worlds.

I was standing in the front of the one of my schools just prior to the start of the school day when our PTA treasurer approached me and asked to speak privately. Once we were seated in my office, behind the closed door, she told me she had been losing sleep over what was going on and decided she had to report it even though she was terribly worried about what might happen. PTA money, she informed me, was being spent on non-school-related things.

"For example," she said, "when the PTA board goes out for lunch, one of the board members always uses the PTA checkbook to pay for everyone's meal."

"Although it sounds like a misuse of funds it doesn't sound unfixable," I assured her.

"Might be as simple as each of you reimbursing the account and attaching a letter of explanation to be included with the bookkeeping materials."

I noticed her hands were trembling as she reached to pull a tissue from the box in the center of the table.

"It's not just that," she said, lifting the tissue to the corners of each eye.

With a quavering voice, she went on to tell me several other PTA account checks had been made out to places like nail salons, restaurants, clothing stores, and local bars.

"If you added all of these checks together," I asked her, "just how much money do you think we're talking about?"

"All of it," she said, reaching for another tissue.

"And, how much is 'all of it'?" I asked, dreading the answer.

"Eleven thousand dollars."

A little boy was sent to the office from recess because another boy reported he'd said a bad word. When asked what he said to the other boy, he looked confused and replied, "All I said was that yesterday my mom made penis brittle."

CHAPTER SIX

"Gimme! Gimme! Gimme!"

EVERY PRINCIPAL SUPERVISES AND EVALUATES HIS OR her school's staff. That generally means teachers, staff assistants (referred to in some districts as teacher's aides, teachers' assistants or para-pros), kitchen staff, specialists, psychologist, counselor, nurse, and custodians.

All schools have their superstars—those teachers who shine. Hallway bulletin boards are amazing; student-made holiday presents for parents are amazing; classroom newsletter is amazing; everything is amazing—including the number of parent requests for those teachers. Sometimes the teacher's instructional skills are also amazing. Sometimes not. Sometimes the teachers who have neither the instinct nor the inclination to look amazing are, in fact, amazing!

When I became an administrator, the first lesson I learned was that it's impossible to tell how proficient a teacher is by his or her friendliness, popularity, or displayed creativity.

Being able to observe accomplished teachers teach is a gift. I remember completing my first teacher observation as an associate principal after which I walked directly into the principal's office and said, "My God, Tammy is an incredible teacher!"

"That she is," the principal responded.

He knew because he'd observed her many times over the years. I'd never before had this opportunity. Tammy was a sweet, unassuming fifty-something teacher who seldom spoke up during meetings. That first observation provided me a valuable lesson and a necessary dose of humility. This teacher, who I later discovered was seldom requested by parents, was a superstar in our building. Her lesson planning was perfection. She flitted about the room helping struggling students and prepared meaningful extension activities for those ready to move forward. Her instruction was so clear, so masterful, that at one point while I was observing I stopped taking notes and found myself just listening. Back when I was in the classroom, I was regarded by administrators and peers as an excellent teacher and I had my fair share of parent requests. Tammy would have put me to shame and I could have learned a great deal from her had we been teachers on the same grade-level team.

By contrast, I worked with a teacher who popped into the office at least twice a week to show off her outfit of the day. She often dressed in elaborate costumes based upon what her students were studying. Her costumes impressed parents and provided the illusion that she was a fun and easygoing young woman. Staff knew otherwise. She outfitted her classroom with almost everything money could buy. The items she'd purchased created a visual explosion of colorful high-interest learning tools. Sadly, these were seldom in the hands of students. The teacher was more of a museum docent than a learning facilitator, as she didn't really like for students to touch her belongings.

If I had one wish for parents, it would be that they trust schools when it comes to placing their children with the appropriate teacher each year. Teachers and administrators do their best to create classes. It's an incredibly complex puzzle. Each child's academic strengths and needs, personality, learning style, and behaviors must be taken into consideration. The goal is to ensure the best learning situation for each child and to create balanced classrooms. Other things have to be factored in as well—the number of potential parent volunteers, the number of students with unique learning needs, students whose behaviors escalate when they are in the same classroom, students who perform well when placed together, etc.

Once in a while, there are some very legitimate behind-the-scenes requests. And, yes, they do come both from parents and from teachers.

"I don't want my child with THAT teacher because she is my ex-husband's new girlfriend."

"Please don't give me another child from THAT family because the mom called all the time and emailed me every single day."

Because I didn't solicit or accept teacher requests from parents, I ended up spending a lot of time explaining why. I had to be the advocate for every child. Sometimes it was a difficult position. I recall a parent stopping by to let me know that a second year with her child's current teacher would be perfectly okay. I had asked the teacher to move up to the next grade level in the fall. She was very agreeable to the idea, but with one caveat. She asked that she not have one particular student in class next year who'd been in her class this year. She had valid reasons for the request. I told her I would make that happen. Ironically, the student she requested to not have in next year's class was the child of the parent who was now asking for her to spend another year with the same teacher.

After hearing my well-practiced response, ending with "I have to be the advocate for all students and create balanced classrooms," the parent did the most unusual thing—she winked. Not a quick shut-tered-camera-lens kind of wink, but an overly exaggerated stage wink, accompanied by an unattractive fish-shaped open mouth and bobbing head nod.

"I trust the system," she said, gathering up her purse and backing her chair away from the table.

She shook my hand, thanked me, and winked again, repeating, "I trust the system."

I'm pretty sure she left totally discarding everything I'd said and just filed it all under the heading of "but this is ME we're talking about." I decided it was best to let her remain disillusioned for the time being and wait until fall for reality to hit the fan.

In checking placement cards for the upcoming school year, I saw that her daughter was not placed in that teacher's class for a second year. I kept my promise to the teacher—which I also firmly believe was in the best interest of the child.

Remember how it used to be? Each school year would end, and on the last day final report cards were handed out. Although they were inside sealed envelopes, we opened ours as soon as we were outside the classroom. Kids would run around asking one another two questions: "Did you pass?" and "Who'd you get?"

Somewhere along the line we decided everyone passes—but that's a whole 'nother book.

"Who'd you get?" meant "who's your teacher next year?"

Today, in many schools, teachers' next-year's class lists can't be finalized in June. Two variables make it difficult to do so. School staffing is more fluid than it was years ago, especially in at-risk schools. Teachers move and teachers quit. Student populations also flex more than ever before. In one of my schools we registered over a hundred and fifty new students within one school year, yet we ended the year in June with only six students more than we began with in September. Schools like this might as well have a revolving door.

In one school, we posted class lists on the walls of the cafeteria a couple of days before school began. On this day, students and their families could come to school and meet the teacher and see the classroom.

Every year, during the first few minutes of this event, I'd go into hiding. Other principals, admittedly, were doing the same thing at their schools. We weren't shirking duties, we were just temporarily unavailable for a darn good reason.

Students were sometimes initially disappointed upon finding out their best friend was in a different class or if they didn't end up with the teacher they'd wanted. Parents were concerned about why their child was chosen to be in a split-grade class or why their child got the new teacher.

If the principal were easily accessible and near the class lists when they were first revealed, he or she would be barraged with requests to change teachers. I was conveniently out of sight for just a short time—say, fifteen minutes.

During those few minutes, kids and parents would enter the new classroom and be warmly welcomed by the teacher. Each student found his or her desk with its shiny new name tag. The freshly-scrubbed classroom had colorful bulletin boards decorating the walls, and—what do you know?—some friends were in the same class. With few exceptions, that's all it took for everyone to be happy. As a principal, it wasn't always what I did that made a difference; sometimes, it was what I didn't do.

It used to drive me crazy when an evening event was approaching and a few parents (usually the ones involved in planning the event) would ask why I wouldn't just "make" all of the staff show up. I repeatedly reminded folks that attendance at skate night, movie night, carnival, bingo night, etc., wasn't mandatory, as they took place outside of paid work hours. I'd put on my best game face and discuss it with them at length—assuring them that, although it's not mandatory that they do, I will encourage staff to participate. Inevitably, someone would say, "But, if they're really dedicated, you'd think they'd want to be there—for the kids."

It doesn't mean they're not dedicated, if they choose to be home—with their own kids (I would be silently thinking).

A primary-level student announced that his family was going to Hawaii for spring break. Asked if he'd ever flown before, he said, "Yes, but this time I think we're going to drive."

CHAPTER SEVEN

"Every Breath You Take"

THE BIG SCREEN FADED TO BLACK AND SOMEONE HIT the light switches to the sound of half-hearted applause. I blinked a few times trying to accustom my eyes to the bright florescent lights and tried to pull myself mentally back into the room.

Coffee breaks during Tuesday principals' meetings were short. The noise level rose quickly because there was so little time. Felt kind of like high school passing time—a few minutes to use the restroom, open your locker, and get to the next class.

Some principals used the time to step outside for a breath of fresh air or to make a quick phone call. Some made small talk with friends. A few would find a trusted colleague to seek some quick advice about an issue back at his or her school.

Looking at the agenda on the table, I noticed that something relating to custodial services was coming up next. I looked at my watch. We're right on time.

Never failed. Meetings lasted from 8:00 until noon, never until 10:50 or 11:49, or until there was nothing of substance left to share. They never started late and never ended early. Friends working in various departments told us they'd be asked to come up with something a day or so before the meeting whenever the agenda wasn't full.

I took my seat at my usual table—nearest the door—and searched through the inside pockets of my purse for a piece of gum. Because I have asthma, I've always had to have a bag of tricks ready to stave off asthma episodes—mouth-moisturizing spray, a bottle of water, a cup of hot coffee, cough syrup, chewing gum, and sitting at a table sans perfumes, colognes, or scented lotions. On Tuesdays, I always sat at a table nearest both the restroom and the exit. Just in case.

One year, during an October meeting, I experienced a significant asthma episode. I began wheezing and felt my airways begin to narrow. Knowing I needed to take care of it immediately, I left the table and quickly made my way to the restroom where I dropped my purse into the sink and pulled out my emergency inhaler. By that time I was coughing and gasping for air, which made it impossible for the first two or three puffs on the inhaler to be effective.

Feeling dizzy and unsteady, I slowly slid my way down the wall I'd been leaning against until I was seated on the cold tile floor. I tried the inhaler once more, again without success. Its dry mist hit the back of my throat and I wasn't able to inhale before coughing it out.

The bathroom door swung open and I looked up to see the tall and slender woman with shoulder-length honey-blonde hair. Although she was a colleague at a school very near mine, I didn't really know her well. But I was sure relieved to see her standing in the doorway.

She said something about helping. Without air, I couldn't speak; so, I just reached out toward her with my hands waving.

"Oh, okay," she said.

Misinterpreting my frantic gestures, she began backing her way out of the restroom door saying, "I'll just leave you be and give you your privacy."

I recall thinking something along the lines of, I'm going to die—in a restroom—on a Tuesday.

Seconds later, my husband who was, of course, also attending the principals' meeting, burst into the ladies' room. He grabbed me under each arm, scooped me to a standing position, and half-dragged me into the hallway just outside the restroom. He then ran back inside to get my purse and retrieve the Epi-pen I always carried. A split second later, he jabbed the pen's small needle into the top of my right thigh—right through my brand-new taupe-colored stockings. Having been through the drill a few times prior, he knew what to do. A colleague of ours, who knew me well, soon realized what was going on and was on the pay phone in the hallway requesting an ambulance.

Sitting on the floor, leaning against the wall, I began breathing a bit easier and was even able to take a small sip of cool water from a paper cup someone handed to me. The wheezing stopped, my body began to feel shaky and jittery, and that horrible feeling that I was drowning subsided. Never before had I been so thankful to feel the epi-pen's effects.

In the distance I heard the siren of the ambulance that would be carting me away in just a few minutes; and, from the room next door, I heard the speaker ask the principals to take out the handout entitled: Custodial Responsibilities.

A fourth grader is speaking to me at the bus-loading zone. "So, you're the principal, right?" he says. "Then, who's that other lady—the step principal?"

CHAPTER EIGHT

"Witchy Woman"

A SCHOOL CUSTODIAN IS RESPONSIBLE FOR THE cleaning and maintenance of his or her assigned building. They are knowledgeable about all facets of the building, including troubleshooting equipment and systems, identifying potential safety concerns, purchasing cleaning supplies, submitting work orders for painting, grounds work, etc.

Their position on the safety team, should there be an emergency, is invaluable. This is the person who shuts off the gas main and water lines and locks exterior doors. In addition to all of this, he or she must perform daily custodial duties—emptying trash, vacuuming, mopping, cleaning up cafeteria spills, responding to those inevitable intercom calls: "Clean-up in room sixteen."

I've been blessed to have worked with some of the best custodians. Top of the list was a tall, rotund man with a deep voice who sported the biggest smile and had the biggest heart. I don't know if he really loved his job but, every single day, he sure gave everyone the impression he did. He entered classrooms softly humming and offered a cheerful, "Hey, my friend, how y'all doin' today?" to each student and staff member he encountered. Our school was always spotlessly shining and he was pure joy. He was diagnosed with cancer midway through the school year. He kept this news to himself until he could no longer work. His funeral, held inside a fully packed church, was truly a celebration of this beloved man's life.

A custodian was briefly assigned to the building I worked in while he awaited transfer into a higher-paying middle school position. Man, he was a multitasker if ever there was one. When responding to a radio call, while walking from one wing to another, he would take the cloth that always hung from his back pocket and use it to dust the length of the bookcase ledge surrounding the library. His gifts were efficiency, organization, and the ability to prioritize. Acknowledging that he was much younger than my dad, I shared with him that him he reminded me very much of my father, who had the most admirable work ethic. Unfortunately, the gentleman was only at our school for a couple of months or so. I sure hated to see him leave. Our paths would cross years later and for a most unexpected reason.

In one of the schools where I was the principal, our custodian left campus in his car during his work hours accompanied by one of our staff assistants. It was after school had let out for the year, but teachers were still occasionally stopping by to pick something up or drop something off. On this particular day, a teacher arrived at the building and was surprised to find the front door unlocked. She went into the office, which was also unlocked, and called for the custodian over the intercom. When there was no response, she became nervous about being alone in the building, so she left.

She reported this to me right away and I drove to the building and locked the doors. The following morning I spoke with the custodian. He told me he and the staff assistant were "involved" with one another. She had walked from her home to the school to see him and he was just giving her a ride home because it had started raining.

I explained that my concern wasn't about his personal life but about the fact that he'd left the building vulnerable to theft or vandalism by leaving during his shift and not locking doors.

"My wife is a lesbian!" he suddenly blurted.

Didn't see that coming and still not exactly sure why he felt the need to share.

I wasn't aware of our evening custodian's affiliation with witchcraft until a spooky encounter occurred after school one day in front of a small audience of terrified teachers. I had sent an email to the woman earlier in the day letting her know she'd been seen (by a staff member) smoking on the school grounds during her break. It was a fairly brief email simply reminding her (once again) of the districtwide "no smoking on school grounds" policy.

When she arrived on campus shortly before the start of her shift, she sat down at a computer in the back of the staff room and opened her email. As luck would have it, she finished reading my email just prior to my walking into the staff room to get a cup of tea.

"YOU!" she shouted, jumping up from the chair she sat in and pointing directly at me.

"You are evil and you deserve to be punished!"

Her volume and dramatic words immediately silenced the room and secured everyone's full attention. She continued her angry tirade, telling me she was a "bona fide witch" and was going to put an "evil spell" on me and that I deserved the bad thing that was going to happen.

To say I was surprised would be an understatement. Never in my wildest nightmares could I have imagined a staff member cursing me with an evil spell. A school counselor I worked with once told me that whenever an unusual event arose, I would say, "Well, this is a first." Well, this was truly a first! Judging from the wide-eyed stares and gaping mouths of the sweet primary-level teachers present in the room at the time, it was a first for them, as well.

The witch went on to tell me this was the only time she'd smoked on campus since I talked to her about it the previous week. I asked her to come to my office so we could speak privately.

She refused and continued—red-faced, voice raised—telling me I shouldn't have messed with her, and no matter what I said to her now it wouldn't help me at all because she was not going to reverse the spell.

"I hate you!" she screamed. "I hate you, and I hate everyone here, and I hate this fucking job, and I quit!" With that, she grabbed her keys from the desktop, made a guttural growling sound, knocked over a couple of chairs on her way out of the room, and hurriedly left the building by way of the kitchen's back door.

A bit shaken, I returned to my office, closed the door, and called human resources to report the incident and seek advice. This was new turf. Never before had I had an encounter with an angry witch wanting to quit her job. Is there a special form for this?

Human resources was able to reach her on her cell phone and asked her to come to their office. She met with them within the hour and very willingly signed a letter of resignation.

In an abundance of caution, the district provided security at our building for the next couple of days until we let out for winter break—just in case.

I hadn't felt well through all of winter break. At first I just chalked it up to the usual educator's illness cycle—work like crazy up until the first day of break arrives; let all the stress, junk food, and lack of sleep catch up with you; get sick on the first day of break; and get better just before school resumes. Ask anyone—it's a thing.

This time was different. I wasn't getting better. I steadily and rapidly got worse. A couple of days before winter break ended, I became violently ill—vomiting bile for hours, experiencing debilitating muscle cramps, chills and high fevers. I was transported by ambulance from my home to a nearby hospital. An emergency room nurse told my family my white blood cell count was similar to what they would see in someone fighting leukemia.

Later diagnosed with a bacterial infection and kidney failure, I stayed in the hospital for eleven days, enduring some pretty invasive interventions and repeated blood draws and scans. Recuperation took weeks, as the illness left me with colitis and an ulcerated esophagus requiring pain medication and a slow introduction to solid food.

The former employee may or may not be a witch and I really don't believe in evil spells. But I have to admit, that experience, followed by the sudden onset of a serious illness—a bit eerie, indeed!

Fortunately, no students overheard the woman's outburst, and, because she voluntarily resigned, the district didn't have to consider disciplinary action or termination of employment.

A kindergarten boy walked up to me on the playground and said "You were my preschool teacher." I told him I never taught preschool. "Uh-huh," he said, "don't you remember me?" I told him maybe I looked like his preschool teacher. "Do you remember Jessica?" he asked, "or Timmy?" "Do you remember that green couch?" "No, I'm sorry," I told him. "You really don't remember where you used to work?" he asked.

CHAPTER NINE

"Take This Job and Shove It"

DURING MY CAREER AS A PRINCIPAL, THREE TEACHERS on staff made personal decisions to resign.

Prior to placement in our elementary school, she'd worked in a public library and as an assistant in a high school library. She'd never worked with elementary students before, and her attitude made it clear she wasn't too pleased about doing so now.

Every day she built on to the barrier she was creating—physically separating herself from the students. She dragged tall bookshelves from the other side of the room positioning them directly in front of her desk. From home, she'd brought two tall plastic palm trees—one for each side of the desk.

Soon after, staff members began noticing other bizarre behaviors. She'd frequently plug her ears with facial tissue and walk around the building with big fluffs of white tissue hanging out of each ear. One day she turned her desk around so it was facing the wall in a kind of self-imposed exile. She asked me if she could clean out a tiny storage closet, adjacent to the library, and put her desk in there. I said no. I was pretty sure if she ever went in there, we'd never see her again.

The library was the center of the school and classrooms were located in wings extending from the library like spokes on a bicycle wheel. This architectural design resulted in students passing through the library while going to and from lunch or traveling to and from special classes, such as art and music. Even though the teachers were doing an exceptional job moving students in quiet, orderly lines, the librarian was complaining about the disruption. I asked for one teacher from each grade level to brainstorm solutions with me. I thought their final idea was a clever and very workable one.

With the custodian's assistance, bookcases were placed end-to-end forming a circle about four feet away from the outer perimeter of the library, creating a walkway around the room (instead of an "X" traffic pattern right through the middle of the room). Students traveled along the edge of the roundabout with their movements fairly hidden by contiguous four-feet-tall bookshelves.

The furniture rearrangement did little to improve the woman's disposition and she came to me within the week with a signed letter of resignation, which I forwarded to human resources.

The following morning I personally packed the contents of her desk and brought them to the office for her to pick up (along with her plastic palm trees). Inside the box, among other belongings, were three rather large and quite sturdy white bras that I'd found stuffed in a bottom desk drawer.

Looking back, I'd like to think she was actually a very nice person whose strange behaviors and sour attitudes were caused, at least in part, by ill-fitting undergarments. Who knows?

For a few weeks, substitutes filled the job, until the district hired a lovely lady who adored both books and children.

The second resignation that year was from a primary-level teacher who was a new hire placed in my building. From the start it was obvious something was amiss. On his first day, he asked me if he could paint the walls of his classroom black. That would be a "no."

Nearly every day he asked to speak with me about problems with "these unruly students." I did several walk-throughs and casual observations, and his first of two formal observations was scheduled to be my first one of the school year. His students didn't seem to know any systems or signals. The classroom wasn't chaotic, but students were confused about expectations and in need of leadership.

At the end of the first month of school, I requested he meet with me and bring his plan book and seating chart. During our meeting I asked him to identify three or four students he felt were not responding to his management efforts so we could brainstorm some ideas.

He immediately said, "Oh, well, for sure Joey."

He opened his planning book to the seating chart and said, "That Russian boy, Pavlev."

"Pavel?" I asked.

He referred to his chart and said, "Oh yeah, sorry, I wasn't sure how to pronounce it."

He told me that two girls talked all the time. "One is named Anna and the other is—just a minute." He looked down at the class roster inside his plan book and his index finger began moving slowly down the list of names.

Before I had a chance to censor myself, I blurted out, "Oh, my God, you don't even know all of your students' names, do you?"

"No," the young man answered honestly. "But, I know most of them, I think."

We two had a lengthy conversation during which I asked questions I wished I'd asked weeks earlier: What part of teaching do you enjoy? What part of teaching do you dislike? Why did you choose to become a teacher? If you were working in a job that is perfect for you, what would you be doing?

His mother, uncle, and grandmother had been teachers. For as long as he could remember, they encouraged him—groomed him—to become a teacher. So, he went to college to become a teacher. What would he be doing if he had his perfect job?

"Working with computers," he said, smiling for the first time since he'd stepped inside my office.

Wow! He not only didn't know his students but this young man also didn't seem to have been allowed to know himself. He had a heart-to-heart conversation with his parents that weekend and on the following Monday he resigned his teaching position to go back to school to get a degree in computer science.

One year, when the number of students entering kindergarten at our school was greater than we'd expected, a new teacher was hired just before the year began. She was a first-year teacher who grew up in San Francisco attending private schools. Her first day on the job did not go well. Neither did her second day, nor third, nor twenty-third. Each day she became more and more frazzled and blamed everything on the students—more than once referring to the children in her class as "unruly animals." She was a bright and articulate young woman who had a sterling academic record. But, in this real-world teaching assignment, she was completely out of her element. She wanted to resign, move back to her parent's house, and apply for a teaching position in a private school. I told her I could see her having great success in that setting.

It's my opinion that every school district I worked in attempted to hire the best, and worked diligently with those who struggled, to help them succeed. On occasions, however, even the most focused efforts fail. The unpleasant duty that follows doesn't fall under the principal's scope of responsibilities. Although principals are often included in recruiting efforts and employment interviews—and are responsible for the supervision and evaluation of those on his or her staff—human resources issues contracts and terminates employment. An employee's potential dismissal isn't a pleasant undertaking for either the employee or the district.

During the first week of school, just minutes prior to dismissal, a teacher rushed into my office reporting two students missing. The teacher insisted the children must have left the line of students while walking back to the classroom from their music class just a few minutes prior.

Both were present for morning attendance. In checking with the teachers who taught reading, music, and art, we determined the children had gone missing sometime in the morning because they'd not been marked present when attendance was taken in any of these three afternoon classes.

We followed protocol—intercom calls asking the students to come to the office, a call to the police, calls to the parents, and a call to the district. All available staff were searching the building and grounds. Upon hearing the intercom call for the two students to come to the office, a girl from an adjoining classroom told her teacher she remembered seeing two students outside knocking on windows after recess. By now, it appeared they might have been inadvertently locked out of the classroom at the end of morning recess and their absence had gone unnoticed by the teacher for the balance of the day.

An interpreter accompanied me to the students' homes as the six-year-olds didn't speak English. We found them each outside their own house, locked out because parents worked. Both were bus riders but, thankfully, were able to navigate their ways home despite the distance and busy streets.

On our way back to the school, the interpreter asked the children, who were now safely belted in the back seat of my car, what happened and why they left school. They both said the same thing—they couldn't get into the classroom after recess. They knocked on the classroom door and windows, but no one heard. Not knowing what to do, the little ones decided to walk home.

Back in the building, I told the police officer, who'd just returned from driving through the school's attendance area, that all was well and thanked him for his time and quick response. The interpreter sat down at a desk in the office to call parents, letting each know their child was safe.

The teacher of the two children, visibly distraught, followed me as I went inside my office to call the district. Suddenly, the door slammed shut and the teacher stood in front of it blocking my exit. Visibly agitated and using a raised voice, the teacher said the children were lying about what happened—which was an interesting claim, since no one had been told what the children said. In the end, this statement would be a key factor in the outcome of the dismissal hearing.

"Sold!" the auctioneer called out, striking his gavel on top of the block of wood on the podium.

"Why in the world did you stop bidding?" my husband asked.

I told him I didn't realize I had.

The same day the two children went missing, my husband and I had planned to attend an evening auction. During the preview, a few days prior, I spotted two beautiful matching chairs I really wanted for our living room—Baker Furniture Company, perfect condition, down-filled cushions. When the chairs came up for bidding I held up my numbered paddle. There were a couple of other bids from the floor and then a phone bid. I bid again. A woman seated in the back corner topped my bid. One of the callers on the phone dropped out; the other phone bidder increased the amount. Apparently the auctioneer looked directly at me and, according to my husband, I just froze. My thoughts, sent reeling back to the unusual and upsetting events of my workday, had momentarily left the auction and now my lovely Baker chairs belong to some stranger on the phone.

A first grader was in the associate principal's office when the doorstop didn't seem to want to hold. Three times the door slowly began to close and each time the associate got up from her chair and kicked the wedge of wood back into the space under the door. The fourth time it happened, the little boy jumped up, began kicking the wood, and said, "Here, let a real man do it!"

CHAPTER TEN

"A Matter of Trust"

J UST AS THERE NEEDS TO BE A SENSE OF "COMMUNITY" within a classroom, and within a school staff, there needs to be a sense of community among principals. Communicating and planning with colleagues can be such an asset yet, in many districts, elementary principals often work in isolation.

I often thought having co-principals assigned two elementary buildings might be an interesting way to build an effective team and capitalize upon each individual's strengths. A principal who's good with budgets, systems, and schedules could be teamed with one whose strengths are instructional coaching and staff development. At any rate, having anyone to team with at the administrative level is a plus.

One team I was on for a few years was the elected group of four administrators who served as a contract bargaining unit representing the district's principals and associate principals. My husband came home from one of the association's after-school meetings and told me I'd been elected president. I thought he was joking because I had never been to one of the meetings. One of my colleagues nominated me and I was elected. So, the next month, for the first time, I attended a meeting.

I approached this task as I would any other. I worked hard at sharing information through explicit but concise communication and was easily accessible whenever a colleague had a question or a problem. In the end, the work felt purposeful and was enjoyable. I especially enjoyed being part of the team that met with human resources in bargaining sessions. Our team was successful in bargaining for increased wages, securing reimbursement for cell phone expenses, adding flexible workdays, and being able to work some non-student and non-staff attendance days from home. I also believe we did this while being respectful of districtwide needs and being able to see the "bigger" picture.

One year the first bargaining session was on Friday, October 30—the same day as my school's traditional costume parade. I dressed as the Queen of Hearts, complete with a full-skirted dress with a red crinoline petticoat, a crystal tiara, and, of course, red high heels.

The meeting at the district office began immediately after school dismissal. So, there I sat, the queen among the suits. A few jokes were made and then we got down to business. Within minutes I forgot how silly I looked.

Another meeting our team of four principals participated in was a monthly sit-down with the superintendent. He told us he wanted to meet monthly to maintain transparency and healthy two-way communication. The first time we met was a congenial small-talk situation. He asked a few questions and told us a couple of things he wanted to do to move our district forward.

The tenor of the next month's meeting changed. The person in charge of budget was there and made a somewhat formal presentation regarding how bleak things would be if our financial ballot measure didn't pass. The superintendent asked us to get the principals on board with donating a portion of their pay (maybe a day or two) to help support the upcoming ballot measure.

The third meeting was drastically different. The superintendent told us about a training in which all principals would participate. This one-man company would provide a multi-day training and we'd be required to use the principals' contractually set-aside funds for continuing education to cover the training expenses. The amount of money was significant and, by contract, ours to spend. I asked if there was any leeway regarding this specific training. Could we look into this training and, possibly, consider alternatives, as well? His response was a swift and terse "no."

As he lifted up the papers lying in front of him and tapped the bottom edge of the stack against the tabletop, sending a nonverbal message that the meeting was coming to an end, one of our principals' association board members spoke up. In a respectful tone, she relayed that the principals were hoping to see the superintendent at Tuesday meetings—at least occasionally.

As she was speaking, the wiry and always anxious-looking man tightly pursed his lips. Then, with brows raised high, he stared at her, eyes bulging, and said, "Don't ever question my moral compass or I'll retreat."

The four of us exited the office, closing the door behind us and saying nothing to one another until we were a fair distance outside of the building. I don't remember who said what first, or exactly what was said, but the gist of our comments was, "What the hell?"

The next month's meeting between the principals' association board and the superintendent was canceled, as were all of the meetings that had been scheduled for the balance of the year.

The following Tuesday we were introduced to the training program we were going to be involved in for the next few months. The guru of the team-building program met with us for several all-day trainings (on days other than Tuesday, of course) which meant more time away from our schools.

The trainer was skillful. His ideas were solid and each training was well prepared and presented. He was in the middle of underscoring the importance of principals working together as a team when I decided to speak up; although, admittedly, I was nervous about doing so.

"I very much agree with what you're saying and value the concept of being a team," I said, "but I've been a principal here for over a decade and I still don't even know the names of about half of the people in this room."

The superintendent, who'd been looking directly at me as I spoke, suddenly looked over at the presenter and made a comedic palm-to-forehead slap accompanied by an audible, "duh!"

The presenter asked those in the room to raise his or her hand if the same was true for them. Almost every hand went up.

Getting to know one another is the first step in building trust, and trust is key to learning from one another. It's true in a classroom. It's true in a school. It's true in a school district.

I asked one of our students if he had brothers or sisters. He said he had one sister who was almost six. "But she's probably going to stay five," he said. "Because my mom said if she doesn't start behaving, she's not going to get to have her birthday."

CHAPTER ELEVEN

"Welcome to the Party"

P RINCIPALS HAVE DIFFERING BELIEFS AND COMFORT levels when it comes to socializing with staff. Some worry it muddies the boss–employee relationship. I think the opposite. In every district and every school my husband and I have worked in, we've hosted staff gatherings—beginning-of-the-year, Christmas, end-of-the-year. We also hosted numerous parties for principals, and, yes, we even mixed in a few district office friends.

We often provided the food and drinks—especially when the staff was on the younger side—as those folks were typically on limited budgets and, let's be honest, no party needs forty-five bags of store-brand corn chips.

How loud and late the parties became also seemed to depend on the average age of the staff. After one party (an impromptu spaghetti feed at our house after a Friday happy hour at a local pub), one staff member ended up spending the night on our family room sofa and another slept in our guest room.

The following Monday everyone acted as usual. Neither mentioned having had a little too much to be able to drive home. Neither did I. We had a fun Friday evening and now it was Monday morning. No harm, no foul. Lots of laughter and good memories; now, back to work.

During a middle-school Christmas party, the noise level was already pretty high when a resounding crash followed by a big burst of laughter suddenly erupted in the kitchen. Someone accidently leaned against the button next to the stovetop causing the retractable air vent to rise. Platters of shrimp and cocktail sauce and baskets of cheese and crackers were sent flying in the air and sliding off the counter. Partiers trying to catch falling dishes ended up knocking off others. By the end of the night, the kitchen looked as though we needed to call FEMA.

During one elementary party, a few staff members sneakily rearranged our pantry shelves. Let me explain. The contents of my walk-in pantry aren't just tidy, they're like in the movie "Sleeping with the Enemy" tidy. It's one small area of my life where I let mild obsessive compulsive tendencies rule. Canned foods are neatly sorted by contents and size and stacked atop one another with labels turned at exactly the same angles. Rices, pastas, and grains are housed in identical wide-mouthed glass containers with contents neatly printed on each chalk-paint label.

The day after the party, I opened the pantry to find (what I considered) complete disarray. Cans of diced tomatoes were mixed in with green beans, and jars of sliced peaches were sitting atop boxes of crackers. A large can of kidney beans was precariously balanced atop a tower of much smaller cans of diced chilies, and the labeled jar containers were upside down, on their sides, or turned around.

Thank God they didn't know about my drawer of alphabetized spices. A system which, by the way, I no longer use because grouping spices by country (Italian, Mexican, Chinese, Indian, etc.) makes so much more sense.

Our school's secretary, and my long-time friend (let's call her Mary) gave away an ornament from one of our Christmas trees during a school's staff party. I've always decorated more than one tree in our home, and one of the trees is always draped with tiny white lights and its branches ladened with dozens and dozens of hand-blown glass ornaments. A few staff members brought their young children to this particular party, which was wonderful, as it did nothing but add to the festivities. One beautiful little girl (let's call her Lucy) was fascinated with a Christopher Radko ornament of a dalmatian with a red ribbon around his neck. Mary, an extremely generous person by nature, removed the ornament from the tree and told Lucy she could have it and could take it home with her.

Mary found me a few minutes later and "confessed" to what she had done, telling me she'd gladly pay for the ornament.

"I just hope it wasn't a special one," she added.

I told her it had been a gift to us from our daughter. She gave it to us the year our dalmatian, Sparky, was hit by a car. Mary's mouth dropped open and her eyes looked so sad. I really hadn't expected her to believe me and quickly told her I was only joking and that it was perfectly okay. She, and everyone within earshot, laughed.

The story of Lucy's gifted ornament circulated throughout the houseful of guests, and more than a few times during the evening a guest would come up to me with an item from our home—a bar of soap, a pair of shoes, a dining room chair—all saying something along the lines of, "Mary said I could have this."

One winter, when bronchitis turned into pneumonia and I was unable to host the upcoming party, one of our teachers (who happened to live quite close to me) generously volunteered to host. On the evening of the staff get-together, a group of teachers wandered over from the party house and had a little fun decorating the outside of our house for the holidays—with long, long ribbons of white toilet paper. And, wouldn't you know it, it rained early the next morning.

The important message in these shared stories is that staff members felt comfortable enough to mess with me. They trusted me. They knew I would find what they did humorous because they knew my sense of humor. They knew I wouldn't be angry or vindictive because they knew my personality and my character.

I always figured we're all just people—people who work together, in really difficult jobs. The more we can do to make one another's lives easier and more enjoyable, the better. I truly believe that, in the end, we will discover that absolutely nothing in this life was more important than how we treated one another.

During Tuesday's meeting, a representative from the curriculum department now stands at the front of the room. She gently moves the projected paper a little to the side, then to the back, then forward again, until it's perfectly centered in the middle of the screen. The principals, myself included, are squirming a bit. It's been a lot of seat time and a long series of seemingly random topics.

Others from the department are moving about distributing more packets of stapled handouts. I always wished that the printed agenda would have some sort of helpful indicator next to each topic, showing exactly what the principals' role was regarding the presentations (e.g., Action required by 11/5, Just an FYI, Share w/staff via email ASAP, or Confidential—not to be shared).

Upon exiting, after every single meeting, one principal would always say the same single word—"Riveting!" Didn't matter how many times he'd said it before, those around him would always smile or laugh. Then, the parking-lot conversations that ensued while principals walked to their cars usually consisted of questions like "So, are we supposed to do something with this?" "Am I supposed to tell my teachers or will the district email them?" "Why did they tell us that now?"

Veteran principals, for the most part, had learned the system. They usually (but not always) knew when something was just being introduced so we'd be "in the know" versus when something needed to be acted upon. The newest principals, however, were like deer in the headlights. They left meetings shuffling armloads of handouts and placed a couple of clarifying phone calls to colleagues as soon as they got back to their school.

I liked to perform handout triage. Some information I immediately entered into my calendar or made a note of it on my iPad. A few papers

I'd carry back to the building to be completed or filed. Those that I pushed to the center of the table were the ones I dropped in the trash can on the way out.

The meetings I attended throughout my career (both as a classroom teacher and, subsequently, as an administrator), in multiple districts, taught me a lot about what to do and what not to do during the meetings I held as a principal.

"Listen up, because I'm going to give y'all some good advice," the computer teacher said to me, in her raspy smoker's voice, after my first staff meeting of my first administrative year.

"Don't call a meeting when y'all can just send an email," she said. "Don't send an email if y'all can just slip a note in my box. And, don't put anything in my box if y'all can just tell me in the hall."

Man, was that ever sound advice! Do as little as possible to communicate as clearly as possible. Don't have a meeting just to have a meeting. Unless it's a non-meeting, that is.

During a conference with the principal regarding her son's behavior, the parent commented, "I think it'd be fun being a teacher," she said. "Do you have to go to college or something?"

CHAPTER TWELVE

"Sugar, Sugar"

OUR ANNUAL STAFF "NON-MEETING" WASN'T PUBLICLY scheduled. Although it would take place during the usual time slot, on what date it would take place within the school year was always a surprise for the staff.

Everyone would arrive, as per usual, and find out there were special treats. They'd grab something to eat and drink—might be homemade cookies and ice-cold milk, or build-your-own banana splits, or a giant bucketful of assorted candy bars, or maybe a buffet of assorted pies—and would then be told the one and only expectation of them for the duration of the meeting:

For the next thirty to forty-five minutes remain in the room. Relax. Visit with whomever you please about whatever you please, and breathe. There is no agenda.

Things like this weren't just for fun—they were necessary. Working in a school is difficult and challenging. The general public would be surprised to learn of the extreme time constraints placed upon an educator's day. In many districts teachers have twenty-thirty minutes to eat lunch and two fifteen-minute breaks (when students are at recesses). Within these breaks they must check their emails, go to the office to check their mailbox, return parent phone calls, get ready for the next lesson, and use the restroom, if needed. Restroom breaks sometimes feel like a luxury. A friend of mine who is a urologist once told me that the majority of patients she sees for recurrent urinary tract infections are teachers. Not surprising.

Staff assistants' schedules generally don't include any time to speak with the teachers who plan the small-group lessons they must teach and usually don't even include travel time to move from one classroom to another. In some districts classified staff (teacher's aides, and such) don't even have their lunch time included in their paid workday. Ironically, for most, there is neither the time to go home for lunch nor the time to go out for lunch; so, they remain on campus and, yet, lunch break is "off-the-clock."

Whether you're a secretary, a staff assistant, a cook, or a teacher, every minute of every day is assigned to a task. Talking to another adult, having no expectations or demands placed upon you—even for just a few minutes—is a good thing.

I always budgeted one full hour for staff members to have lunch during non-student-attendance staff workdays. The first year in one of the schools where I was principal, a kindergarten teacher re-entered the meeting room after returning from his lunch.

"I just want to thank you for letting us have an hour for a leisurely lunch," he said. "That was very professionally respectful."

I never forgot his words; they made me realize how even something so little was so appreciated.

People joke that you could put a tray of anything (even dog biscuits) in a school's staff room and the tray would be empty by noon. I never tested the dog treats theory; but I have watched people happily dig into cookies, cupcakes, candies, and the like, without regard for where they came from or who made them. Could have been made by the student's parent who ended up on the six o'clock news when the county health department called animal control and thirty-eight snakes were removed from their house. True story!

Candy was the number one favorite treat of the staff at every one of my schools. Somedays I'd put a single *Hershey's Kiss* in everyone's mailbox. *Pay Day* candy bars were the perfect choice for the first payday of the school year—until peanut allergies became so prevalent. Clear plastic gloves filled with popcorn and *Hot Tamales* for fingernails, tied with orange and black curling ribbon, and a plastic spider ring, looked great reaching out from inside all of the mailboxes on Halloween. *Take Five* candy bars were attached to a little note about spending spring break's five well-deserved days to focus on relaxing and renewing.

On the first day of spring staff members would find a vase containing a big bouquet of cookie flowers—flower-shaped cookies attached to the end of wooden skewers by colorful sugar-coated gumdrops.

Bagels (with cream cheese) or *Krispy Kreme* doughnuts were always a welcomed treat when left on top of staff room tables. At each school I also kept a big bowlful of wrapped candies in the principal's office for staff to freely help themselves.

State testing baskets, filled with student answer sheets, test booklets and freshly sharpened No. 2 pencils, also had a treat for the staff member overseeing the test—a *Skor* candy bar. Those pesky end-of-year task sheets were placed in folders with a *Nestlé's Crunch* affixed to each and "It's Crunch Time!" written across the front of every folder.

The first really hot day near the end of the school year is usually pretty unpleasant. Some schools have air conditioning. I worked in three that didn't. Without air the feeling can easily move from unpleasant to miserable by the end of the day—especially for teachers in classrooms with thirty fourth or fifth graders who've just come in from recess. Then, the classroom is not only hot but, also, smells a bit dog kennel-ish.

Every year, sometime around late May, I'd make a trip to Costco to buy several boxes of *Häagen-Dazs* ice-cream bars (and a couple of boxes of juice bars for the non-chocolate or non-dairy folks). These would remain in the school's kitchen's freezer until that first really hot day.

When that hot day arrived, after students departed, the school secretary would announce an impromptu all-staff meeting in the library. They knew what that meant! Like children dashing out the front door upon hearing the ice-cream truck's musical tune, everyone would hurry down the halls headed for a very welcome cold treat.

At one school, an intermediate-level teacher popped her head in the office while eating the last of her ice cream.

"You know, several of us guessed that today was going to be the ice-cream day," she said. "It's what kept me going when it was eighty-five degrees in my classroom!"

Attendance in every district was supposed to be turned in by a specified time each morning. I always felt bad for the school's clerk when she had to call several classrooms to remind the teacher his or her attendance hadn't been turned in yet. I felt bad for the teachers, as well; because back when I was teaching, I remember receiving plenty of those calls myself.

We finally hit upon a way to successfully decrease the number of late-arriving attendance folders. On the first day of each month, a large container filled with candy—*Hershey Kisses, M&Ms, Starbursts, Smarties,* or *Jolly Ranchers*—was on display in a central location. Each class would turn in their daily guess as to how many treats were in the container—inside their attendance folder. The catch was, if the attendance folder was turned in late, that day's guess didn't count.

Attendance folders were returned to the teachers later that day with a blank attendance roster with a small arrow drawn next to where tomorrow's guess would be written. An arrow going up indicated today's guess was too high. An arrow in a downward direction meant their numerical guess was too low. On the last day of the month, the container of treats would be delivered to the class that guessed the number correctly or guessed closest to the actual number.

A school's staff needs as many things as possible to look forward to and lots of little traditions to help them make it through the year, the month, the week, or—let's be honest—sometimes, the day. My husband

and I always both felt the same; the school day went by quickly and the school year went by quickly, but the time between Monday and Friday seemed to last forever!

Parent-teacher conference days were an example of a time staff really needed a morale boost. Those days (and the days preparing for them) could be exhausting. Teachers looked forward to meeting with parents to discuss their students' progress. Typically, they were well-prepared, had work samples to share, and had communicated with parents enough so that nothing shared during the conference would come as a surprise. Nevertheless, every year there were a few conferences I'd be asked by teachers to sit in on. My job wasn't to say or do anything—just be there—in case the conference took a turn for the worse.

During parent–teacher conferences, some of the information shared was exactly the same for all students—homework policy, an upcoming major assignment, etc. By the second day, "Did I already tell you this?" was a question teachers asked as they began to feel like a recording.

For many years, at one particular school, the secretary and I pooled our efforts to provide dinner for the staff during conferences. Somehow, she always convinced a local restaurant to donate the entree. I'd make a trip to Costco to buy several pumpkin pies, whipped cream, Romaine lettuce, Caesar dressing, lemons, and bags of croutons. On the afternoon of the long conference day (that extended well into the evening), we'd use the school's kitchen to reheat the main course and make enormous bowls of Caesar salad. Staff would self-serve pumpkin pie with whipped cream.

It warmed my heart to hear all the talking and laughter escaping from the staff room door each time someone walked in or out during dinner breaks.

In truth, working in schools today is a completely different game than when I began my career. We never had intruder-alert lockdowns or active shooter trainings. We didn't have to give thought to where we could hide children if a bad guy entered the front door. There was no state-testing mandate. Teachers had more autonomy and permission to express creativity. Children's behaviors (with rare exceptions) were far more manageable, and parents almost always supported the school (again, with rare exceptions). Teaching is harder today.

As a teenager, I always volunteered to be on the planning committees for homecomings, dances, convocations, proms, etc.; and, as an adult, I'd planned and hosted a good number of theme parties through the years. It's no wonder I loved planning staff meetings and workshop days that always included team-building games, quick-paced, meaningful learning activities, and, of course, food!

The first staff meeting of each year was always my favorite. Principals throughout the country spend time with staff on one of those first fall days going over their district's required information and training. Because each district allocates resources differently, in some I had as little as half a day and, in others, as much as two full days to accomplish this task.

The most important thing about that first meeting is that it sets the tone for the rest of the year. For this reason, I looked at information that needed to be imparted the same way I looked at learning in the classroom. How can I make the learning achievable, interactive, and fun?

One year, during our back-to-school all-staff meeting, everyone reviewed district policies and information by playing a video Jeopardy game in teams.

"Do not make advance travel plans for these," the board read.

"What are designated snow make-up days?"

During another first-of-the-year staff meeting everyone received a printed study guide containing policy changes, expectations of employees, health and safety guidelines, etc. They spent time studying the information together in teams after which everyone took part in a "pop" quiz—batting around inflated balloons that each contained a piece of paper with a written question on it. Using safety pins the balloons were popped and each team shared and answered their questions.

One year, to review back-to-school information, staff participated in a competitive scavenger hunt throughout the building. During another September's first staff meeting, to learn policy changes and review employee expectations. everyone played a quick-paced game of "college bowl" (with an assigned kazoo blower at each table—in place of buzzers).

When I wanted to introduce the concept of "bucket filling" to my staff as a building-wide vocabulary, I shared the books "*How Full is Your Bucket*" and "*Have You Filled a Bucket Today?*" by Carol McCloud and Katherine Martin. Upon entering the room, each staff member was handed a small bucket. In the center of the room there was a huge bucket filled with assorted wrapped candies. The staff voted to implement the concept and use a shared vocabulary to help students understand that through their actions and words they can help themselves and others to feel happy.

When "team planning" was the identified goal for the year, we spread vinyl tablecloths upside down on the gym floor. Teams of ten people stood on each cloth. The goal was for each team to try to be the first to turn the cloth right side up. Three rules: no talking, no touching the cloth with your hands, and everyone must keep one foot on the cloth at all times. Of course, it took a while, but, finally, one team figured it out. Then, they did it again, but this time they could talk to one another. Because they were able to plan together, all the cloths were turned over in no time.

For another activity, long rectangles were marked on the floor using painter's tape. Inside the rectangles were several mousetraps placed in random positions. Each team's goal was to guide one blindfolded member of their team through the maze of mouse traps without springing any. It was quickly discovered that not everyone could direct at once.

One year, when "the ten research-identified components of an effective school" were to be shared with staff, we broke into ten teams. Each team planned and presented their assigned one component of effective schools in a way that would help us remember. Pretty easy to remember a beautiful painting of a mountaintop being held up while the team sang "Climb Every Mountain" (setting goals). Pretty impossible to forget seeing a team surround one of its team members as each of them kept providing him additional support—a band-aid, an ace bandage, a sling, a crutch, and even an athletic supporter (supportive work environment).

Playing "Teams Games Tournament" was a fun and fast way to go over district and building information that needed to be shared. Grade-level teams studied questions and answers together. Then, each team sent one member to each of the game tables. So, around each table there was a representative from each grade level. They'd pull one question (the same ones they had just studied) from a basket, and whoever's turn it was would try to answer. If they answered it correctly, they won the strip of paper to take back to their team. If they needed to call on someone else at the table for help in answering, the player and their helper would each get half of the strip. Players would just keep going clockwise around the table answering until all of the questions were gone. Everyone would then take the strips they'd won back to their original study teams. Whichever team collectively won the most strips was the tournament's prize-winning team.

One of the most meaningful activities, according to teacher feedback, was when we arranged for substitute release for each grade-level team (one team at a time) to work for an entire day rewriting their grade's math standards. The goal was to understand the standards clearly enough that we could rewrite them into kid-friendly language. Our math specialist, our school improvement facilitator, and I were present at each team's workshop. These standards were written by the state and, surprisingly, the vocabulary was difficult enough that in the first hour of the first day we were searching for math dictionaries. One grade level realized they had been assessing students' mastery of one particular standard completely wrong.

When all grades had completed their workshops, we met as a staff to decide where to go from there. Everyone was in agreement that we needed posters for the classrooms so teachers could refer to the standards prior to and during lessons to help students know what they were learning and how achievement would be assessed. So, I put in an order to have posters made.

The next day I received a call from my supervisor asking what the hell I thought I was doing. The order for classroom posters was cancelled and I was told not to use the fruits of our labor. These were state standards and we had no right to rewrite them, I was told.

Two years later an activity, recommended by the state, was to engage teachers in rewording their grade's standards so kids could understand what they were learning and how learning would be assessed.

It's not enough just to have a good idea; the timing has to be good, as well.

A first grader who only spoke English was fully convinced he understood Russian. He couldn't. But occasionally we'd call him to the office to have him "interpret" for us. (Admittedly, for our own amusement.) A Russian-speaking child would say something to him and our little interpreter would say something like "He wants to know what's for lunch" or "He wants to know how much minutes until recess."

CHAPTER THIRTEEN

"You Need to Calm Down"

I N EVERY CLASSROOM, THERE IS A WIDE RANGE OF personalities, issues, and behaviors. There might be a class clown (or two), a shy student, and an overbearing student who wants to answer every question. There might be a bully, a child who has difficulty controlling anger, a generous child who helps others, and a really, really loud child.

It's not much different with any group—even among staff and among parents.

During my years in administration, most of the parents of students were delightful. They seemed appreciative of our work, respectful of our expertise, cooperative with our decisions, and supportive of their children's academic achievement.

I only experienced a small number of parents' explosive tempers. There was no commonality in terms of the economic standing, education, or appearance of these individuals. They were simply adults who, for whatever reasons, hadn't yet learned to manage their anger in ways that were appropriate and effective.

While working as one school's assistant principal, I was fortunate to be mentored by a very wise principal. His soft southern accent and gentlemanly manner reminded me of Andy Griffith's television character Sheriff Andy Taylor. Many times, during that first year as an administrator, I felt like a wide-eyed Opie listening to Pa's sage advice.

I sat with him in his office, one time, while a woman ranted for nearly forty minutes. When she finally began to wind down, the principal asked her if she would excuse him while he stepped out to get a drink of water. He stopped in the doorway, turned back, and said, "You know what? Coffee sounds better. Can I get anybody else a cup of coffee?"

To my surprise, the parent said in a much calmer tone, "Yes, please—sugar, no cream."

While he was out of the room, I asked the woman if she had other children and she asked me if I had children. I asked where she grew up. She complimented my shoes.

The principal returned with coffee for her and for himself, and the secretary followed closely behind with a cup of tea for me. Just the way I like it—with a spoonful of honey.

Not until then did the principal take out a pen and paper. He took a noisy sip of the steaming coffee, smiled, and said, "My, that's nice!"

Then, he asked the woman, who sat calmly sipping coffee, "Ma'am, what did you hope to have happen when you came to see me today?"

She hesitated for a few seconds and then told him she just wanted him to know what had happened in the classroom. She said she didn't want her son moved to another class and wasn't sure she wanted him to tell the teacher about her visit. She just wanted him to know.

He told her he was going to make a note of what she said happened. He thanked her for calling it to his attention and said his hope was that he'd file it away and she wouldn't have any concerns the rest of the year.

Then, he said if she ever did have a concern, she's always welcome to visit with him again.

She thanked us both and she left. Amazing! She. Just. Left.

Fascinated by what I'd just witnessed, I asked the principal a few questions. I wanted to know why he let her carry on for so long. He said she'd most likely practiced in her head all of the things she was going to say. She was prepared to spew it all out so, might as well let her.

"Sometimes," he said, "if you stop them in the middle, they'll just rewind the tape and start over."

In the end, he told me, it probably would have taken longer if he had interrupted to ask questions or tried to calm her before she was ready. When I asked why he didn't take notes, he said it would have been a waste of time. She couldn't tell him what she really wanted until she had worked through her own emotions enough to know what she really wanted.

"Was the coffee run just to calm her down?" I asked.

"Nope. I just wanted some coffee."

"One more thing," I said, "why did you ask me to come in here with you?"

"Are you kidding?" he said with a grin. "That woman scares me!"

The term "helicopter parent" has been around for a long time. Usually—but, certainly not always—it's the mom. The helicopter parent seems ever present. She's at school frequently and is in constant contact with the teacher and principal via phone and email. She hovers around her child and might even do some of his or her schoolwork and home-work. We had one lady who'd shout out answers, before the students even had a chance, whenever the teacher asked a question of the class. The helicopter parent either doesn't completely trust the school with her child or doesn't completely trust that her child can thrive without her. There is a cure for the helicopter parent—it's called middle school.

By contrast, the "stealth bomber" stays away from the school for extended periods of time and then, one day, just swoops in unexpectedly and starts firing away.

I had a "stealth bomber" experience after changing the lunchroom dismissal system. Previously, students had been allowed to dump lunch trays and go to recess when they decided they were finished eating. Problem was, we had quite a few who were choosing to dump full trays. They wanted a longer recess more than they wanted to eat lunch.

I decided to post a very visible time schedule in the cafeteria. When each grade level's twenty minutes was up, students could raise hands to be dismissed. Those monitoring the cafeteria would wander around and quickly dismiss complete tables by saying, "Push your chairs in and this table may be dismissed."

After the second day of the new system, a parent came to my office to let me know her daughter wanted to go back to the old system. She didn't like having to sit there with her hand up. Her mother agreed with her and felt it was demeaning. She should be able to finish her lunch and just dismiss herself.

"Did you involve the students at all in making this decision?" the bomber asked.

I explained the timetable and that all grade levels had a minimum of twenty minutes for lunch. I also explained many weren't eating their lunches and were overloading the playground with too many students at a time—which was a safety concern because there was neither the supervision nor the play equipment to handle more than one grade level at a time during recesses.

We talked for half an hour until she was finally satisfied it was a good decision. Upon leaving, she turned at the door (*ready*). "You know, coming up with a new system wasn't the mistake," she said, (*aim*) "but you should have fully explained the reason for it to the students." (*Fire!*)

Another challenging parent that educators occasionally encounter is the one with an unrealistic picture of their child's performance or behavior at school. These are the parents of the child who "never lies," and "would never use such language," When called about a disciplinary issue regarding their child, this parent inevitably asks, "Well, what I want to know is what did you do to the other kid?" To this day, that question baffles me. Being a parent myself, I was concerned with my own child's development and growth. Asking about the other kid is akin to picking up your car from the garage and asking the mechanic, "Well, what I want to know is what did you do to the other cars?"

When people are embarrassed or angry, sometimes they say things just to feel like they are more in control of the situation. I finally came up with a response to the one comment I disliked the most: "I pay taxes, so you work for me."

It was usually said by the parent of a suspended student. While it wasn't at all effective, it still happened—kind of a last-ditch effort to try to make me change my mind. In the final year of my career, a very bullying man leaned forward and began aggressively pointing his index finger at me as he was exiting my office and, there it was, he said it.

"Yeah, well I pay taxes, missy, so you work for me!"

"I'm a taxpayer, too," I responded. "So, applying your logic, I'm actually self-employed."

When a boy said to his friend, "I'm gonna kill you!" while arguing about a four-square call on the playground, the student who said it was sent to the office and was suspended for one day. I asked the counselor to speak with the other boy. He reported to me later that there didn't seem to be any issue. The student said he wasn't afraid of the other boy and said he knew he was just mad because he didn't think he should be called out. It was nearing the end of the day and I had three other disciplinary referrals to deal with. It was my intention to call the parent of the boy who'd been told "I'm gonna kill you" before leaving the office. The boy went home and told his parents, so the father called me.

He started the conversation yelling.

"I am going to take this to the school board and demand that you be fired!" he screamed into the phone, after which, unfortunately, I could clearly hear the sound of a toilet being flushed.

"My child's life was threatened, and you didn't even give a damn," he yelled.

The two boys knew one another well and were friends. I had taken action, there were consequences, and I made sure the other boy felt safe. I have a feeling I would have been screamed at by the father even if I had called him first.

That night I dreamed about the man's phone call. Waking a little after 4:00 A.M., I felt so rattled I simply turned on the faucet thinking a soothing bath might calm me. Sitting in the warm water of a bubble bath I began sobbing. I truly wasn't sure I wanted to do this job anymore. Not so many "thank-yous" and way too many "fuck yous."

But I dried my swollen eyes, got dressed, put on my makeup and a smile, and did it all over again. Meanwhile, the man either calmed down or found another target for his wrath because I never heard from him again and he didn't call the school board demanding I be fired.

When I called to tell the mother of one of our students that her son had threatened to beat up another boy and he would be missing recess tomorrow to solve his problem in what we call the "solutions room," she immediately became angry and defensive. She wanted to know if the kid he threatened would be missing recess, too, because he must have done something first to have made her son so mad.

I assured her we would get to the bottom of it and that's what the solutions room was for. It wasn't punitive; it was to help kids solve their problems. She started yelling, telling me her son didn't have problems.

"I'll tell you the problem," she shouted, "you've got your head up your ass, that's the problem!"

Here I thought the problem was her son's behavioral choices and, come to find out, I had an anatomical abnormality. Who knew? My end of the conversation went pretty much unheard because of her angry yelling, so I decided to employ a trick another principal told me about years before—hang up on myself. You don't do it while the other person is talking because then you're hanging up on them. You start talking and just hang up mid-sentence. I tried it.

"Well, tomorrow he will just come to…." *Click.*

My God, it worked! She most likely assumed we got disconnected and probably didn't want to talk to me any more anyway, so she never called back. Even if she had, it would have disrupted the frenzy and maybe allowed a bit of calm-down time.

In the principals meeting, the safety officer was now presenting. He was talking about restraining orders and referenced an incident at my school. A parent had climbed the fence during recess and was distributing explicit handouts about a sex offender in the neighborhood. Staff on recess duty reported it to the office right away.

I went outside, collected the handouts from students, and asked the man to come into the office. When we were seated, I reminded him about the "no trespass" rule and how he needed to come into the office, sign in, and get a visitor's pass. I also told him that all handouts had to be preapproved.

Upon hearing this, his anger level went from zero to ten in a flash.

"I welcomed your fat ass to this school and all you do is cause me trouble," he yelled, grabbing his stack of handouts and rushing toward the door.

Several minutes later, the outer office's main phone line rang and this same man asked to speak with me. Apparently, he had more to yell. He told me he'd be on campus whenever he wanted and didn't have to follow any of my goddam stupid rules.

"Your days are numbered, lady," he said in the most menacing tone before slamming down the receiver.

I called the district to report the incident. Later that afternoon the district called me to let me know that the city police went to the man's house and issued a restraining order.

A little girl was swinging her backpack trying to hit her brother as the two waited to board their bus. "Hey, what's going on?" the associate principal asked. "I'm mad at him!" the girl announced. "Make him stop calling me by my neck name!"

CHAPTER FOURTEEN

"Drowning in the Swim of Things"

I NEEDED TO MOVE. I GOT UP TO REFILL MY COFFEE CUP. Both coffee urns were empty. Looking at my principal colleagues seated around the round tables, I wondered who else was having a hard time paying attention. One woman had her hands just above her open purse, which was sitting in her lap, and was discreetly taking off each of her artificial fingernails and dropping them inside. A man seated toward the back held his iPad at a low angle. I couldn't see his screen, but the subtle sweeping motion of his index finger made me fairly certain he was playing "Angry Birds." An older principal at the side of the room leaned his head back against the wall and was trying his best to keep his eyes open. A woman sat at the table in the middle of the room, slowly eating a large banana—her usual meeting-day snack.

We hit the midpoint of the principals' meeting, and a colleague seated across the room from me raised her hand to get the speaker's attention. The speaker (the elementary principals' boss) finally saw her hand and called upon her. The principal recounted several unwarranted verbal attacks she'd been experiencing from a student's parent. As she spoke, her voice became increasingly shaky, her eyes welled with tears, and her face reddened until it nearly matched her hair color. She concluded by asking earnestly, "I guess I'm just wanting to know, as a principal, how much abuse do I have to take?"

"All of it," our boss told her.

"All of it," she repeated. "That's the job."

The room fell quiet.

I don't know what anyone else in the room was doing because I was trying to ease my own discomfort by pretending to focus on the stack of papers that had accumulated in front of me during the meeting—busily shuffling through the handouts as though their content had suddenly garnered my full attention.

How much abuse? All of it—that's the job. Knowing that was an honest response didn't make it any less upsetting for the woman who'd posed the question, or for the rest of us who'd personalized the answer knowing, at any point in time, any one of us could be the target of verbal and emotional abuse.

The principal, who by now probably wished she'd never asked the question, was using the pads of her fingers to gently wipe her overflowing tears. She looked so sad, flanked by two female principals who were comforting her with soft whispers and gentle pats on her back.

Without skipping a beat, we moved on to the next agenda topic: swimming. For years we had a primary-grade swimming program because a wealthy community member donated a building and two swimming pools to our district. Making sure children learned to swim was a particular passion for the man who'd amassed a small fortune in the food industry.

We all engaged in our usual mumblings and grumblings about how disruptive swimming was to our reading and lunch schedules, how it was so costly for buses to transport kids to and from the pool locations, how they came back to school with wet hair, how there was no district oversight in the showers and locker rooms, and the fact that most of them didn't learn to swim, anyway.

Our supervisor, a tiny woman with a huge personality, was known for her caustic humor and tendencies to process quickly and answer abruptly. We could already see by her expression that she was ready to abandon the topic and forge ahead. But what instantly quieted everyone was her response to our objections.

"I know, I know, I know. Trust me… I know." She added, "But you know what? The school board wants swimming. So, you all better act like you mega-give-a-shit."

We laughed. How typical of her was this answer. She didn't try to persuade us with research or reason. She just cut to the chase with a touch of sarcasm to let us know this was non-negotiable.

We moved on.

A kindergartner was in my office, waiting for his mother to pick him up. Pointing to a large basket of children's books, I said, "Sweetie, you can read any of those books." In a very excited tone the boy said, "I can? Wow! I didn't know how to read books before!"

CHAPTER FIFTEEN

"Bridge Over Troubled Water"

TUESDAY'S TOPICS DETERMINED THE PACE OF THE meeting—in terms of whether the time felt like it moved quickly or felt like it dragged on forever. Human resource topics were often interesting. Today was no exception: documentation.

The amount of administrative time and paperwork it takes to document personnel issues is substantial. I truly believe this is why lesser concerns are often left unaddressed.

In one school, I'd arranged for teaching teams to have a day of uninterrupted planning with the ELL (English-Language Learner) teacher. They were planning for the following year—creating workable schedules for student groupings and teacher trainings. The ELL teacher was fully trained in GLAD (Guided Language Acquisition Design), a research-proven instructional system using visual and auditory strategies to help ELL students learn through chants, songs, charts, etc.

We were set for success—ready to move into the next school year—when a heavy hammer fell, rendering all of our previous work useless. Human resources informed me our ELL teacher was going to be transferred so my school could absorb a more senior teacher excessed from another staff. His position had been grant-funded and the principal decided next year she'd use the portion of the grant that paid for his salary and benefits in another way. This resulted in his moving into the pool of available teachers, and his seniority exceeded my young teacher's.

I met with his former principal to ask if he was a good teacher.

"Well," she responded, "he's mediocre, at best."

"Did you document any issues?" I asked, knowing it was the only way to dodge a sub-par candidate.

Her unexpected response was "No. I'm sorry, I can't help you there."

Admittedly, I chose to look away when a behavior or an attitude was a "one off" and wasn't representative of who an employee was as a person or as an educator. Sometimes, however, issues were so significant that there was no looking away. They had to be reported, investigated, and, when necessary, addressed.

After December's report cards were issued, I received a phone call from the mother of one of our students. Her child hadn't brought home a report card and, according to her, he was insistent the teacher hadn't given him one.

I fully expected the teacher would tell me he'd been given his report card and that his mother would call right back to say she found it crumpled up in the bottom of his backpack.

Instead, the teacher said, "Oh, yeah, I think I did forget to do one for him."

Still, not a problem, I thought, requesting the teacher go back to the classroom to retrieve the grade book so we could sit down together, average his grades, and complete a report card.

Just minutes later I was handed the gradebook. As I flipped through the pages, I was shocked to see so few entries. It was nearly empty. Science had just one entry per student. In some subjects there were letter grades in some boxes and simply check marks in others. I asked the teacher what a check mark represented and was told it was an "A." The answer was quickly changed to "it just means they turned the assignment in—so maybe it is more like a "C." Unbelievable! There was no record of what an assignment was—just dates. There was no way to know if an entry represented homework, classwork, or a test. I asked the teacher to go back to the classroom and get the lesson plan book so we could reconcile grades with assignments.

Just a few minutes later, I was flipping through the plan book's pages. They reminded me of every diary I attempted to keep as a little girl.

September's first three weeks had been filled in with the task, objective, page numbers, etc. By the end of October, the symmetrical squares had brief notes (Ditto 7 and 8, page 46). November and December were blank pages with the exception of the reminders of a field trip, picture day, and an assembly.

I didn't even try to mask my shock. I asked what was being taught each day. The answer was disturbing. The teacher simply ran off a day's worth of worksheets for each subject.

I said I needed to keep the grade book and plan book for now and would be contacting human resources.

I had once before brought this teacher to the attention of human resources. Several times a squirrely little boy in class was told he was going to be duct-taped to the chair to keep him from getting up. One day the child brought a roll of duct tape from home and gave it to the teacher. As the class cheered, the teacher securely duct-taped the child's legs and torso to his chair.

I used to tell teachers that one of their professional goals should be to never be featured in a YouTube video. If the duct-taping had been videoed, it surely would have gone viral. Even though the boy supplied the tape, and, reportedly, giggled the entire time while being taped, it could have been a disaster.

Human resources provided a cursory "don't duct-tape anyone to furniture ever again" lecture. This time, however, was different. I believe to teach with no lesson plans and to not maintain accurate progress records amounts to educational malpractice.

The teacher and a union representative met with the HR director and me. The teacher claimed being overwhelmed because of a particularly difficult class and promised to do much better in keeping accurate plans and records.

The HR director came up with a consequence. From that day forward (until further notice), the teacher was to turn in plans for each week's lessons, dropping them in the box outside of my office every Monday before school. I would review the plans, making any necessary notations or changes, and would walk the book down to the classroom before the start of school.

This went on for six weeks. Six very long weeks. I told the teacher not to bring plans to me anymore but made it clear that I could, and would, at any time, ask to see the lesson plan book and grade book. The problem was addressed, and corrective measures had been put in place and had been met.

Whenever a problem or concern is brought to the principal's attention, it requires thoughtful action. The unspoken rules are: Don't ignore. Don't overreact. CYA (cover your ass).

When an anonymous letter was passed on to me, via the office clerk, it took only a moment for me to decide the right thing to do. The unknown author of the typewritten letter was reporting that a teacher on staff was addicted to methamphetamine. The letter's author identified the teacher by name and claimed the teacher was an addict.

I'd known the teacher for over a decade. Never had there been issues with absences or tardiness, nor issues regarding instructional skill or relationships with students and staff. The teacher looked strong and healthy and had beautiful teeth (not so with most meth addicts). I would have bet my year's salary that what the letter claimed was false and I so wished I could just shred it. But it wasn't my job to determine the truth or the outcome. It was my duty to report. So, I hand-carried the letter to human resources.

A representative from human resources called the teacher in to discuss the letter. Again, now that they knew, they had no other choice. The teacher denied the accusations and that was that.

I always felt terrible about having to report this. In the aftermath, the teacher was mature and professional and completely understood that we were all just doing our jobs.

Two fifth-grade girls came to my office to tell me about a male staff assistant they felt was being rude to them. Both were native Russian speakers, who, although they were learning English, still had some significant grammatical gaps and very heavy accents.

With the help of a Russian-speaking interpreter on our staff, they were able to clarify that they felt he was inappropriate with them because he said their breasts were getting big.

They were both visibly upset and both insisted that was what had happened.

I asked them if they could say, in English, exactly the words the staff assistant said to them.

"You girls are getting big," one of the young ladies responded.

Then, the other girl pointed to her chest and said, "They call these 'girls,' you know."

Okay. Made perfect sense. The staff assistant was commenting that the girls (not their breasts) had grown over the summer. No bad intentions. Simply words—lost in translation.

A teacher's assistant (who had the most seniority in the district) was standing cafeteria duty one day. She leaned over and whispered in my ear, "The girls were pretty good today; but the boys kept holding the corn dogs under the table near their crotches and wiggling them around. God, I hate corn dog day!"

CHAPTER SIXTEEN

"The Fool on the Hill"

THE MEETING ROOM WENT DARK. ANOTHER HUMAN resources representative stepped up to the document camera and adjusted her paper until it was perfectly square on the screen behind her. Looks like the topic's the interest registry. Teachers wanting to make a move for the following school year (to another building) put their names on the interest registry in the spring.

Some of the teachers on the registry are involuntary moves resulting from the forecasting of a lower number of students at their schools in the coming year. The teacher with the least seniority in the building is moved. Some go on the registry just for a change. Some want to move to a school nearer their home. There are always a few "frequent fliers" on the registry, as well—the ones who repeatedly bounce from one school to another.

When principals open the registry for the first time, we immediately look to see who wants to come to our school and who wants to leave. Statistically, some schools are more desired work sites than others. The list is long for the schools in higher socioeconomic areas of town where test scores are typically higher and discipline issues are typically fewer. Teachers often let principals know if they're going on the registry. It is just a courtesy to help them in planning for the following year. I opened my email one day and noticed a string of emails from staff members with subject lines relating to "next year" or "interest registry."

The first one was from a teacher who was part of the original staff when the school opened. She said she and one of her teammates wanted to team-teach social studies and were both going on the interest registry for middle schools. Although I was disappointed, I could see them maybe wanting to do that.

The next email was from a special education teacher who said she was applying for a couple of schools where the discipline wouldn't be as difficult and time consuming.

Another email let me know one of my teachers wanted to move to my husband's elementary school across town because it was closer to her home.

After the seventh email I knew I'd be getting a call from the district wanting to know why so many were wanting to leave my building. In their eyes, this kind of mass exodus couldn't help but be a direct reflection upon my leadership. Other principals had shared that such things were brought up during their evaluation meetings.

I hadn't known until that morning that anyone was leaving. Our staff was a very stable one. I thought these particular teachers were happy in their assignments. More than a little confused, I wondered—what I could have done, should have done—to keep them on board.

Later that day, the secretary, whose desk was located near the printer, shared with me that each time I exited my office to pull another sheet of paper from the printer, I looked sadder and sadder. With printed copies of all of the emails in hand, I headed from the office to the wing where most of the teachers jumping ship were located. As I swung the wing's door open, I look down at the email at the top of the stack and just happened to notice the date: April 1.

"April Fools!" the students' voices rang out in unison as I passed by the open classroom doors.

I was never so glad to be the butt of a joke. They absolutely got me and I was ever so thankful no one was actually leaving. We'd built a strong team.

I, by chance, shared an historical moment with one of our team members. On the day of Barack Obama's presidential inauguration I scurried to the library and found a seat near where it was playing on the television. I didn't want to miss it. This was history in the making. It was even more moving than I'd imagined it was going to be. A black man was our President. A black man would be living in the White House—a building built by black slaves.

I felt a lump in my throat and my eyes filled with tears. The hopefulness, the possibilities—I felt like I was drowning in my own emotions. I was glad I hadn't chosen to step into one of the classrooms to watch the inauguration, as I had usually done. This one was different. I looked around to see if there were any boxes of tissue on the tables. I didn't see any, but to my surprise, I spotted a teacher seated alone at a table across the room. She, too, was wiping her teary eyes.

This was a teacher I'd known for quite a while. She was an excellent teacher and I both admired and liked her very much. At the time, I didn't say anything and she didn't say anything. But, I was so glad to know that I'd shared this special moment with someone else and was very pleased that it was her.

A little girl came into the office and the attendance clerk told her, "Honey, your shoes are on the wrong feet." The girl responded, "These are my shoes." "I know," the clerk said, "but, they're on the wrong feet." "Nah-uh," the girl answered, "these are my feet, too."

CHAPTER SEVENTEEN

"The Life that's Chosen Me"

THE PROCESS OF IDENTIFYING A STUDENT FOR SPECIAL education services or for alternate placement is complex—as it should be. We'd never want to rush the process and misidentify a student. But extreme outbursts and violent behaviors are challenging for educators.

One Halloween morning, I overheard three teachers in the work room talking about a student. They were saying he needed to be moved to self-contained classroom for students with severe behavioral issues. That year we happened to have several students whose behaviors were very difficult to manage. This kind of talk was increasing enough that I decided to write the following message on the back of the staff's weekly bulletin:

> *Tonight, most of our students will put on a disguise and go door to door "begging" for a treat. For some of our students, it's kind of the same way at school every day. Children wearing "disguises," move*

from situation to situation, and from person to person, "begging" for attention.

Some disguises are pretty hard for us to see through—the emotionally fragile child who wears a disguise of indifference, an abused child who disguises fear and anger with inappropriate humor, a child affected by substance abuse who wears a mask of aggression. The list of "costumes" is as lengthy as the list of issues. Some are endearing enough that the attention they attract is mostly positive. Others will take any attention—including negative. They'll take the trick over the treat.

Recently, there's been quite a bit of conversation about some of our students. That's appropriate when the intent is to gain understanding and share strategies with those who work directly with the student. Conversation centering around why students with issues are allowed in school, speculation about mental illness, etc., aren't in the best interest of the student. Many times, our staff works magic and a student succeeds so well that today's child doesn't behave as he did a year or two ago. But, sometimes, our school isn't the best placement. We'll discover and document this by honoring the process. Public discussion won't speed the process; it does, however, have the potential to apply lasting labels to the student and to drag us down, as a staff. Our daily jobs are difficult. Exposure to or involvement in perpetuating negative talk would only seem to make them more so.

In college, teachers were often told, "Speak to your students as if the child's parents and the school board could hear you." If this is the standard of professional dialogue we hope to achieve, the same would hold true when we're speaking ABOUT students.

While working within the system, our challenge is to safeguard confidentiality, to do that which is in the best interest of the child, and to remind ourselves that the most repellant masks are often worn by the children who need us most.

At the end of dismissal, I returned to the building. Folding the umbrella and slipping my arms out of my long black coat, I headed to the office to stash them back inside the closet. To my surprise, five teachers were seated at the round conference table.

"Can we talk with you about this?" a third-grade teacher asked while waving a copy of the bulletin she held in her hand.

After a short discussion it became clear that she and each of the other teachers in the room thought the letter was addressing them personally because of recent negative conversations they had engaged in about various students. I explained that the problem had become pervasive enough that it needed to be addressed with all staff. I told them the fact that not one of them was on my radar, yet they had all stepped forward with worry, proved my point.

I wanted to be the cool, beloved principal in red high heels. Pretty quickly, though, I realized that at any given time, someone is going to be upset with my decisions or actions. It's the job.

From the first day of school one little child was struggling terribly with the simplest of tasks in the classroom. We even needed to escort the student from the bus to the cafeteria each morning because the student would get lost if we didn't. Once referred for testing, the parents agreed, as they were witnessing a great many difficulties at home as well.

The day arrived for the parents to meet with our team—the school psychologist, special education teacher, classroom teacher, and me. The couple entered my office pushing a stroller in which their infant child slept. It took them awhile to get settled, positioning the stroller in between their two chairs.

The psychologist shared information about the testing that would occur. The classroom teacher shared a collection of the child's work samples, and we discussed the student's strengths and areas of concern.

When the parents were asked to share information, the mother reached down and picked the baby up from the stroller and held the still-sleeping child right in front of her face and whispered to the father, "What should we tell them?"

She then passed the infant over to the father, who also used the infant to shield his face from us, "I don't know," he whispered back, "I don't know what to say."

He held the infant at arm's length so the mother could take her.

"I thought you said we wouldn't have to talk." the mother said to the father.

This back-and-forth shielded and whispered conversation continued for a few more minutes while everyone else seated around the table remained silently stunned. The classroom teacher discreetly got my attention—and, perhaps for a reality check—made a slight gesture pointing toward the parents and mouthed the words, "We can hear them."

"Yes," I nodded and silently mouthed back, "yes, we can."

It felt slightly reminiscent of a Will Ferrell *Saturday Night Live* skit, but, in fact, we later discovered we were communicating with two parents who themselves had challenges.

They loved their children and were doing their best for them. However, we needed to really step up our game by fully explaining everything, breaking it down into manageable chunks of information and providing visual examples.

"Pink tray! Pink tray!" was a daily request in the cafeteria of one school.

A child with autism would, every single day, perseverate about being able to get a pink lunch tray. There were twenty times more green trays because the pink ones were leftovers from a batch that had been purchased several years before.

Understandably, the student didn't want to be handed one but wanted to take it from off of the stack like the other students did. And, of course, it had to be pink. Bless their hearts, every day the cafeteria workers would hurriedly count how many students were in the queue ahead of this child who was the entire time frantically calling out, "Pink tray, pink tray, pink tray!"

As the little one moved closer and closer to the stack of rigid plastic trays, the student would become more and more flustered. The staff would have already slid a pink tray into the stack—at exactly where it needed to be for it to end up being taken from the top of the stack by a now very happy child.

Jerry slinked along the perimeters of rooms and peered inside open doorways with one eye—hiding much of himself behind walls and door casings. Often he would he slink his way to my office door. Because he had an articulation issue, he would greet me with, "Hewo, Mithis Weawy."

He was the sweetest little boy, but so non-productive he drove his teacher crazy. In a meeting we asked his mother and father what he likes to do. He loved using tools to take things apart.

We made a deal with Jerry. By doing school work, he could earn time to take things apart.

His teacher gave him his completed work to show us on his way to lunch. We'd get him all set up in the conference room with tools and something to take apart during lunchtime recess. I donated my Sony Beta Max to the cause along with a cassette player—not like I needed them anymore. Other's brought unwanted items for Jerry to disassemble. When we ran out of machines and small appliances for him to take apart I made a couple of trips to Goodwill.

A little boy was escorted by his teacher to my office each day. For some reason, the non-verbal child was fascinated with trash cans. As a daily reward for good behavior his teacher took him on a "trash can tour" of the school. Each day I had a piece of trash ready for him to crumple and toss into the can. If he showed up earlier than I was expecting I'd sometimes resort to giving him a blank sheet of paper. He'd crumple it up tightly, toss it in, smile and, then, wave before exiting the door.

"See you tomorrow."

Sadly, never a response.

Some of our little ones had histories of abuse or psychological or emotional issues, and this sometimes translated into greater behavioral challenges for them. One school I worked in housed one of the district's "behaviorally challenged" classrooms. The teacher, who did an amazing job of calmly de-escalating angry children, wasn't having success one day with a particular student who needed to be removed from the group. The teacher escorted him to the small time-out room inside the classroom and stood with his back against the door (which could not be locked) to prevent the child from exiting. He turned around a few minutes later to check on the student through the narrow window in the door. The student had completely stripped down, was pointing toward his penis with both index fingers, and, although he couldn't be heard the teacher could read his lips as he yelled, "Suck my dick."

At another school, day after day, a student would smear his feces all over the stall wall in the restroom. The student would even throw feces upward so some would be found clinging to the suspended ceiling tiles like foul-smelling stalactites.

This behavior is very unusual. It's not a prank or a misbehavior or meanness. Clearly the little one had significant issues and we needed to work diligently, together with the parents, to gather information and to figure out how best to help.

One day—after it hit the wall—I captured some photos using my personal camera. My intent was to add these photos in with the assemblage of data and information for our upcoming meeting.

That evening I dropped the film off at a local drug store (obviously at a time before digital cameras). A few days later, I asked my husband to pick up the prints, completely forgetting what I'd photographed. In addition to the poop pics there were about thirty pictures of individual pairs of shoes each posed in pretty positions in front of a white backdrop. I had this idea to affix a photo to the outside of each pair's closet storage box to make it easier for me to locate the pair I wanted to wear each day.

At the drug store counter, while the clerk processed his credit card transaction, my sweet husband opened the envelope and started shuffling through the pictures expecting to see some vacation memories. He quickly picked the prints up from the counter and pushed them back inside the envelope and left the store. When he got home, he told me that if the FBI is looking for a suspect who has a fetish for poop and ladies' shoes, he's doomed.

At the end of the year, students sat in a circle as their teacher led them on a trip down memory lane. Each took a turn sharing what he or she remembered fondly about the year. Switching gears, the teacher then asked her fourth graders to look ahead and share if anything made them nervous about next year. One by one they spoke of increased homework, not knowing everyone in next year's class, etc. Then came Vladimir's turn. "I'm afraid," he said, in his thick Russian accent, "that I'll have to marry an American woman!"

CHAPTER EIGHTEEN

"Memories"

NEAR THE BEGINNING OF MY CAREER, I WAS ASSIGNED to a particularly challenging school. The student population had outgrown the small structure and student behaviors had escalated significantly during the last few years. The former principal left his office just as if he planned to return the following day. He packed nothing—his half-filled coffee mug left sitting on the middle of the desk. My first task, at the end of summer and before staff and students arrived, was to clear out the office. My predecessor was a stamp collector. Stamps were everywhere—in drawers, in files, on the floor. I boxed his personal belongings—stamps, photos, files, books and his now-washed coffee mug—and sent them by courier to the district office.

That school happened to be the school within the district boundaries that was the farthest away from my home. That distance was a blessing. On the way to school each day, I listened to either the comedy channel or the smooth jazz station to kind of mentally prepare myself for whatever the day would bring. I drove a convertible back then. What an amazing feeling it was at the end of a hard day to retract the top, and feel the air blowing against my face and through my hair. It was absolutely energizing. One day, while on my way home, I noticed a car full of high-school-aged boys had suddenly pulled up from behind and abruptly changed lanes so their car was right next to mine on the freeway. They were all looking my way and one of the boys was leaning way out of the back window and waving both arms. As I looked over at them, their wide smiles erupted into open-mouthed laughter and they started playfully pushing one another's shoulders. The kid who'd been hanging halfway out the window quickly ducked himself fully back inside the car. As the car sped past mine, I realized what probably happened.

They saw a shiny new convertible driven by someone with long hair flying in the wind. Being boys, they were checking it out, only to discover the driver (me) was older than their mothers. The joke was on them. Unexpected reminder of the passing of time—that joke was on me.

After the end of one of our Tuesday meetings, one of my fellow principals noticed I had a new convertible. It was absolutely pouring that afternoon. In the parking lot, in front of a large group of principals, he yelled out, "Hey, Karen, I'll give you five bucks to put your top down."

Walking toward my car, I called back, "For five bucks, you'd better be talking about the car."

Principals sometimes need to transport students in their personal vehicle. For example, when a student is ill, suspended, misses the bus, has live lice and, for whatever reason, the parent can't come to school to pick him or her up. Whenever I had to drive a lice-infested student home, I insisted he or she wear one of the cafeteria's hair bonnets. Of course, I would wear one too, so the child wouldn't feel bad.

One day I was driving a little boy home because he missed the bus (again). He looked all around, seemingly fascinated with the top of my car.

"Mrs. Leary," he asked, "are tent cars cheaper than real cars?"

Just for fun, I twisted the front latch and let him push the button that controlled the retractable top. He was so excited watching it fold into place.

A few days later that same little boy was entering the crosswalk where I was standing duty. He yelled out to me, "Mrs. Leary, remember when you drove me home and we took your top down?" I looked around at all the parents, students, and staff nearby and quickly said, "I drive a convertible."

That school made for a treasure trove of unusual memories. There was the time someone walking on the path adjoining the playground mooned the fifth graders during recess. Then, there was the time kids shattered the front windshield of my car after I asked them to not skateboard on school grounds. A fist fight broke out during the PTA family dance. The two fighting mothers had been arguing over whose daughter's shoes had higher heels.

There was the parent who, when filling out a volunteer clearance form, asked if she could explain something on the back of the form. I told her to go ahead.

"About my felony," she wrote. "The only reason it was first degree robbery was because the guns was stolen."

Oh, okay. Understandable.

One morning when one of our first-grade teachers was on her way to the classroom, she spotted a mouse running across the library floor. When she came into the office to report it, I assured her I'd let the custodians know.

Every day from then on she would inquire, "Did they catch that mouse yet?"

Before long, word spread, and others in the building were talking about "that" mouse. The night custodian was setting traps when he arrived, and the daytime custodian collected them in the morning before anyone else arrived.

Before the end of the week, four or five had been caught and the nesting location was determined to likely be in the staff room where three were trapped. The area was thoroughly searched. When the day custodian moved the dingy old sofa away from the wall, it revealed an abundance of mouse droppings. Flipping the sofa forward, exposing its underside, he discovered mice had pulled out the polyester stuffing in some areas and bunched it up tightly in other areas. The white filling was heavily dotted with mouse droppings and the fabric lining had been almost completely eaten away.

When the night custodian arrived, the two men carried the sofa outside and dropped it next to the dumpster—letting it fall hard on the asphalt.

In their retelling, they claimed that when it hit the ground, a huge plume of dust arose from out of the old piece of furniture, they heard the wood frame crack, and several mice who were still hiding amidst the springs and stuffing scattered in all directions. They continued to set traps for a couple of weeks and steam cleaned the staff room carpet twice.

Good news was we were finally able to say, "Yes, they caught 'that' mouse."

Bad news was, after school the same day, the school's office clerk saw a pickup truck belonging to one of our student's families pulling out of the parking lot. Sticking out well past the closed tailgate of the truck was the old staff room sofa, headed off to its new home.

During our careers, my husband and I often worked at dissimilar schools. While I worked at one of the largest schools in one of the most affluent areas of a big city, he was the principal of one of the district's smaller at-risk schools. At another district, when he worked at a school having some of the highest test scores and an excellent attendance rate, I worked at a school that had among the lowest test scores and high absenteeism.

In the evenings we would tell one another about our days. Through the years one of us would be disciplining for issues like blurting out in class or not doing schoolwork, while the other's day was filled with students telling the teacher "fuck you," stealing from the book fair, or fist fights at the bus stop. Whereas one of us spent time during the day talking with police officers, the other might have had a lengthy meeting with parents and their attorney. Doesn't matter where you work, all principals' jobs are challenging and difficult work. The primary reason for this is that we're not working during the 1950's.

A fourth grader rushed into the office yelling, "Get the janitor! There's shit coming out of the toilet." Our well-meaning secretary asked, "Can you think of a more appropriate way to say that?" The boy replied, "Get the janitor. Shit's coming out of the toilet, please."

CHAPTER NINETEEN

"Stayin' Alive"

THE SUPERINTENDENT STOOD AT THE FRONT OF THE meeting room announcing we were now on an (air quotes) "official" break. Everyone knew what that meant. This wasn't our first rodeo. We remained seated.

The school district's financial measure was on the upcoming voter's ballot and that meant we all had duties assigned to help it get passed. A schedule was distributed showing the dates and times of each school's phone bank night—for which we were supposed to get several staff members and volunteer parents to come with us to call registered voters to encourage them to vote.

We were also told when and where the envelope stuffing events would take place. Then, there were also the yard signs. We'd each be given a number of signs to give to staff members and volunteer parents to put up in yards of willing community members.

We'd also be expected to go door to door leaving voter information fliers in our assigned neighborhood.

This time a couple of new ideas were floated. The superintendent wanted to pass a paper around and have each of us write our names on it followed by all of the clubs, organizations, churches, etc., that we were members of or affiliated with. The purpose was to make sure we were covering all areas in town to promote the levy. The paper sat on the first table for several minutes. It was passed to the next table, and the next. When it was passed on to the table where I was seated, I saw only a few people had written anything down.

I was relieved because it felt weirdly invasive. I passed the paper on without writing anything.

As the paper was being circulated, we were also asked to each donate a minimum of $50 to the ballot measure fund to help pay for postage, yard signs, and such. This didn't feel right. It didn't feel like a choice; it felt mandatory. Looking around the room it was pretty obvious by facial expressions and shared whisperings the idea wasn't sitting too well with other principals, as well.

I was president of the principals' association for two years. As the outgoing president, I discussed it with the incoming president, who was sitting across from me at the same table. She announced at the end of the meeting that in lieu of individual donations, the principals' and associate principals' organization would be making a generous donation on behalf of all principals. The (air quotes) "break" ended and we continued with the regular agenda.

It was sunny. Bright light streamed through the glass entry doors and more than anything I wanted to push open one of those doors and stand outside and feel the sunlight shine on my face.

For some reason, the urge to go outside and the sunlight reminded me of another very sunny day during another Tuesday meeting. We'd only been in session for an hour when our school's secretary, looking very shaken, entered the meeting room (highly unusual!). She whispered into my ear that before-school recess ended and two kindergarten girls (who were waiting in the office) reported seeing a "big guy on the playground with a gun."

"Put us in lockdown," I said. "Call 911."

She ran out of the building to follow my instructions. I quickly gathered my belongings from the table and moved to the other side of the room, where my supervisor sat sipping her black coffee. After being briefed of the situation, she, too, quickly gathered her belongings and accompanied me to the school.

Back in the building, the secretary was on the phone speaking with a 911 dispatcher. Classrooms were already locked down. Blinds were closed. Doors were locked. Office personnel were monitoring teachers' on-line verifications of students who were present and those who were missing. The custodian was locking all exterior doors.

The SWAT team swooped in so suddenly and soundlessly it resembled a tense scene in a crime drama. The first officer to enter happened to be a close family friend. Head-to-toe black, drawn weapon, and serious demeanor made him and the others look both intimidating and reassuring.

My friend's focus was so much on the job (as it should have been), he showed no sign of even knowing who I was, other than being the principal of the school he was helping. The team spread out and scattered, stealthily moving through the building, making hardly a sound.

Two officers remained in the main office. One focused on the kindergarten girls—asking them to tell him only what they were sure about.

"How big is the boy? Is he bigger than the kids at your school? What color is his hair? What was he wearing? Did he tell you he had a gun or did you see a gun? Show me with your hands how big the gun was."

The other officer asked me if anyone had recently been suspended? Had anyone made threats? Where do the students store their backpacks?

My supervisor and I were busily sweeping in the late arrivers and housing them in the health room. Prior to the police arriving, when a few very young students became confused and afraid to stay inside the building, we both told them to hurry to their classroom because we were having a safety drill. Office personnel were notifying teachers via email that their late-arriving students were in the office and were safe.

Parents outside the school, who'd just dropped their children off for the day, were beginning to park cars and gather at the front entrance of the school. They could tell something was going on—something wasn't quite right—and we couldn't open the doors to explain.

Television news crews arrived amazingly fast, armed with microphones, cameras, and questions. News vans parked across the street from the school and reporters were trying to get the attention of parents to interview them.

That night our school was a feature story on the evening news, and the next morning it made the front page of our newspaper.

In the end, thankfully, it wasn't as big a story as the journalists had anticipated it might be. Neither the fourth-grade boy nor the "gun" was a threat to students or staff. It was a toy gun—a cheap plastic squirt gun the student had tucked into his pocket and brought to school.

He briefly took it out of his pocket during recess and aimed it at some students before shoving it back inside the pocket of his hoodie.

The kindergarten students did exactly the right thing by reporting. Our school did exactly the right thing by locking down and calling 911. When it comes to keeping students and staff safe, it's better to look a fool than to be a fool. Assume the worst and take action.

During our "after-action review" with the district safety officer and office staff, the safety officer said we shouldn't have told children that it was a drill because it wasn't. It was true, both my supervisor and I had said it was a drill to a few very young students who were afraid because of the commotion. During the debriefing the safety officer said he heard that I told some students it was a drill and I should never do that if it's a real lockdown situation. I said I saw his point but, at the time, I was just trying my best to accomplish two things quickly: calm the students and get them inside. My supervisor said nothing. I actually was the first to say, "Don't be scared, it's just a drill." I said it first and she repeated my words and my mistake.

After school that day, our counselor, clerk, secretary, and I met to discuss what happened. We identified one huge misstep that was overlooked during the after-action review—a safety protocol concern that needed to be addressed right away. Why did the secretary run to the building contiguous to the school to tell me about the incident? Why didn't she, herself, put the building in lockdown and call 911?

Excellent questions. Time was lost. Had there been a real gun and a potential shooter, lives could have been lost.

Although she expressed feeling terrible about her judgement, this misstep was not the secretary's fault. Clearly, it was mine and mine alone.

Having spent nine years at that school, I was instrumental in developing our safety plan, in training staff, and in leading every drill. I was always the one who made the call to lock down.

All along, we should have been having numerous drills during which I stepped completely aside so others would step up. Fires, intruders, earthquakes, and such don't conveniently happen only when the principal is available to orchestrate everyone's movements. They can, and do, happen at any time—even during a Tuesday meeting. Responses from parents and the neighborhood were extremely positive. Numerous phone calls and in-person chats let us know they were thankful we took the reported incident so seriously and didn't hesitate to call the police.

The television news announced a phone number viewers could call to voice opinions. This was interesting. A couple of people thought the principal should get a raise or be promoted for acting quickly. A small number thought we overreacted and the student shouldn't face consequences. One guy said the custodian should be fired. No, I don't understand that one either.

Most spoke of being saddened by today's teachers and parents having to worry about shootings. Lots of "what's our world coming to?" sentiments were expressed.

Wasn't too pleased our school was getting all this attention. The incident certainly didn't merit front-page newspaper coverage or being the lead story on two local news channels. But, they had the footage, the photos, and the story—so, they ran with it—probably because nothing worse than this happened in our city on that day. So, that was the good news.

As a direct consequence of our own "after-action review," we immediately conducted emergency drills adding in unusual factors. We put "door is on fire" signs on some exits to find out what students and staff would do if they had to alter their usual exit routes during an emergency. We called lockdowns during recesses. During the busiest time in the cafeteria, we sounded the fire alarm and, to our surprise, watched as some students pushed in chairs and lined up to dump lunch tray contents in the garbage and recycling bins. Again, we identified a glitch and then retrained staff and students and practiced to overcome the problem.

That following school year, we had a SWAT team visit even before school opened. It was one of those August teacher workdays, when teachers were setting up their classrooms.

One teacher, who was all ready to move into her new portable, had to shift gears. Her books and personal teaching supplies had been moved from her former classroom and were stored in one side of the portable. I was informed that morning the portable wouldn't be ready by the time school started. While awaiting wiring, a few repairs, and the issuance of an occupancy permit, the class was going to have to be situated in the library. Staff members rallied to help their colleague by carrying everything stored in the portable back inside the building and into the library.

On my second or third trip from her portable, I cut through the office where I was startled by a tall man dressed in black carrying an automatic weapon. I stood there, frozen in place, as it took my mind a couple of seconds to recognize the man was a SWAT team officer.

He held his finger up to his mouth, signaling for me to be quiet, and then he leaned forward and whispered, "There may be an armed man in the building."

My first thought was—yeah, you!

Behind me, I could hear a couple of teachers walking down the hall, talking and laughing. I quickly ran back and signaled for them to be quiet and pointed to the officer. The officer led the three of us into the office health room, where four teachers were already sitting silently with the lights turned off. As more and more staff members were ushered into the small health room, the room became more crowded and much warmer.

We couldn't call any classrooms or office spaces because if there really was an intruder, he or she might hear the phone ringing and, even worse, hear it being answered. Two SWAT team members asked me to accompany them as they did a sweep through the building so I could identify what was behind each door before they opened it. So, I did. Art room, music room, electrical room, restroom, and on and on. Each time one of the men threw a door open, the other officer would step in front of me as a shield. I remember, at the time, thinking how back during all those college courses, they sure never prepared me for anything like this.

In the end we discovered someone had called the police saying they saw a man with a rifle walking into the school. No one was ever found and we couldn't see anything unusual when we reviewed the security cameras' footage.

It was a difficult day for everyone; but, for one of our first-year teachers it was especially trying. She pulled into the parking lot just as the SWAT team arrived. One of the officers told her to get back in her car and stay down, which she obediently did—for quite a while longer than the building search lasted. When she worked up enough courage to peek out of her car windshield, she discovered hers was the only car left in the parking lot.

In the Tuesday meeting, the safety officer was informing principals that a large wheeled trash receptacle would soon be delivered to each building. Each would be filled with emergency supplies and equipment.

Someone mentioned bottled water, and it was suggested this would be good to have on hand in case of an emergency, and maybe each PTA could provide that. Then someone suggested we might want to consider purchasing and storing juice instead because it would have vitamins.

The conversation that ensued reminded me of the marble meeting. Several years prior, when I was completing my administrative internship, I led a staff meeting in which the main topic was marbles. Marbles was a pretty big playground activity for kids that year, and some of the staff assistants and teachers wanted to establish common rules.

Should they be allowed to play for keeps? What if there were some students who didn't want to play for keeps? Should they be allowed to keep marbles in their desks? What if we had a chart in each classroom and kids could sign on it to indicate they are "play for keeps players" or "non-keep players?" What if we had designated areas so there's no confusion—like games played to the right of the swings means they're playing for keeps.

"Wait a minute," a fifth-grade teacher interrupted to ask, "has this 'playing for keeps' stuff been a problem at recesses?"

"Well, no," a staff assistant responded. "But what if it did become a problem?"

There were a few giggles as people realized we were trying to micromanage the solution to a problem that didn't even exist. We tabled the discussion, and there was never any need to revisit it, as there wasn't any issue regarding marbles for the balance of the school year.

Tuesday's principals' meeting discussion was continuing. Should we have an assortment of juices? Do they need to be refrigerated? Where should we store them? Should they be in a central location or should they be stored in each classroom? What's the shelf life for juice, anyway? Does it matter if it's in cans or cartons?

After several minutes, one of the veteran principals spoke out, "Who cares? It's not like we're going to have a major emergency and everybody's going to be like 'hey, let's have juice!'"

So much of our job is planning and scheduling to avoid foreseen problems, sometimes we can get carried away coming up with systems and it's good to be pulled back into reality—so we don't start to feel like we're losing our marbles.

So often what we deal with as school administrators relates to student safety. In every school I worked in, there was need to improve the dismissal pickup system. Morning drop-offs were always a piece of cake. Parent pulls up to the entrance, child exits the car, parent drives off.

Dismissals are different. Parents and students arrive at different times. Parents have to locate their child (or multiple children) in the midst of a crowd of exiting students. The children—being children—are usually more focused on talking with friends than watching for parents.

At one school there were two long one-way lanes in front of the school curving in toward the school from the street and back again—kind of like a giant two-lane circular drive. The lanes could get so backed up at dismissal that some impatient parents would park their cars in the lot and yell and motion for their children to come to the car. The kids would then run to the parking lot, across the two lanes of arriving and departing cars. We needed to come up with a system before someone got hit.

I asked a district safety officer to come to the school and watch dismissal with me. We sat down immediately afterward, and for nearly an hour discussed a number of possibilities before arriving at what appeared to be a simple, workable system.

Each day, everything was put in place forty minutes prior to the dismissal bell. Using ordinary orange traffic cones, we blocked the entrances to the staff/visitor parking lot. The cones in the roadway narrowed—funneling the two lanes into one lane—allowing the outside lane to remain open so cars that had loaded could pull out. No more double parking and blocking people's exit.

The teachers stood bus duty, and staff assistants stood duty at nearby crosswalks. A number of staff—our nurse, counselor, and psychologist—graciously agreed to stand carpool duty. I stood in the middle of the crosswalk right in front of the school's entrance to block cars whenever staff or students needed to use the crosswalk. And, yes, I was nearly hit a couple of times and several times "flipped off."

When the staff assistant whose duty it was to put the cones in place was out ill one day, we discovered our carpool system was completely "cone dependent." If the cones were there, everyone followed the rules. If the cones weren't there, it all reverted to a free-for-all.

One woman refused to follow the "please keep pulling forward" suggestion. I'd written a column in the school newsletter explaining the new system. It also explained why it was so helpful to have cars pull forward. When a couple of cars ahead pull out, it just makes sense to pull forward. That way, the end of the car line isn't sticking out into the main road. It's kind of the same as in a long drive-up window lane at a fast-food place. Just keep moving forward.

"Fuck you!" wasn't the response I had expected, although I had by then heard it so many times that I would often just smile and say, "You're welcome." Let 'em wonder if I misheard.

Two days in a row this woman said, "Fuck you," when I asked her to please pull forward. On the second day, however, waving her finger in the direction of the staff parking lot, she added, "Just wait until I find out which one of these cars is yours."

I told her I was going to issue a "no trespass letter" to her because of her language and inferred threat. This meant she wouldn't be allowed on the school's property until the next quarter.

The following morning, the woman appeared in the office and asked to see me. She apologized and asked me to reconsider her not being allowed on the school's property.

She said the issue was gasoline. She came to the school and parked and she couldn't afford to keep the car running or to keep turning the engine off and on to pull forward. Within the past month she lost both her job and her boyfriend. She had been fired for missing work when her youngest child was sick. Her boyfriend had been killed in a drive-by shooting.

She said that seeing me standing there all dressed up with my pink lipstick and red high heels, smiling and saying, "please drive forward," made her furious. But she said it had nothing to do with me and everything to do with all of the other stuff. We hugged before she left. I gave her some gas money and connected her with an organization that helps community members.

A lot is asked of people these days. Teachers feel they have to use their own money to outfit their classrooms—which, in many cases, is pretty much true—and parents feel they're expected to foot the bills for supplies that were previously included in a "free and public education." Also, true.

One day in early September, right after the end of school day, the secretary told me an angry parent was on the phone. It was about the supplies list. On the phone she said something about sending pencils and a box of facial tissue to school today. Apparently, the teacher told her daughter it'd be better if she could bring in everything on the list at one time instead of a couple things each day—a message the daughter relayed to the mom when she got home today.

The woman was yelling on the phone—not raising her voice—yelling! It was difficult to speak with her because she just kept repeating herself. At first, I thought the issue was that she was angry with the teacher. But, by now, something was telling me her anger had nothing to do with the teacher or the school. Several times she used the expression "this is the last straw."

"You keep saying *the last straw*," I said. "What were some of the straws leading up to this?"

After the auditory relief of a few seconds of silence, she asked, "Why do you care?"

"I don't know," I said. "Maybe I can help."

Again, she was silent for a couple of seconds and I could tell she'd started crying.

During the balance of the call, I learned that two weeks prior she was diagnosed with breast cancer. Her ex-husband was laid off last month and hadn't paid child support this month. The owner of the house she was renting told her he's going to sell it, so now she needs to look for a new place to live. Her daughter was late for school that day because she missed the bus. She drove her daughter to school—which made her late for work. And, the last straw, was when her daughter got home and said the teacher preferred to have all school supplies sent in at once.

"Well, I'd like to use what little money we have left this month for food—that's what I'd prefer," the woman said sarcastically.

I told her I'd written down her address and would be arriving at her house in about an hour because I had something for her. I said I'd honk when I got there (pre–cell phone days), and she could just come out and meet me at my car.

From our supplies closet, I hurriedly gathered all of the supplies that were on the list—pencils, crayons, paper, scissors, Elmer's glue, colored pencils, erasers. I figured those were the supplies we used anyway whenever parents couldn't provide them. This mother (and her child) needed the dignity of being able to send supplies to school more than we needed to have them stockpiled in the bins on our closet shelves.

Our school had a wonderful partnership with a large church that was located a couple of blocks away. They reimbursed us for family hardship purchases for things such as children's shoes, gas, and groceries. Usually, they approved gift card purchases in advance. I decided if they wouldn't approve these retroactively, I would just pay for them myself.

After a quick stop at the nearby market to purchase a grocery gift card and a gas gift card, I headed for her house. Just one quick horn beep and the woman exited the door. She was younger than I had expected. She looked tired and troubled. Who in her circumstances wouldn't?

I told her I was sorry to hear she and her family were going through difficult times and suggested she have her daughter bring the bag back to school in the morning, as it had all of the supplies on the list. As I handed her the gift cards, I explained they weren't from me or from the school but were from the Baptist Church. Her eyes welled up with tears, and she quickly walked back toward the house. Just before stepping inside, she turned and mouthed the words "thank you."

I recall thinking how blessed I was to be in a position to be able to help her. School personnel are often "in positions to help others." Countless numbers of teachers I've known keep snacks in their classrooms to feed hungry students. They pay for these snacks with their own money and shop for them on their own time.

I've known teachers and staff assistants who have purchased clothing and shoes and paid for haircuts for students. I've seen staff go to the cafeteria and pay for a student's overdue lunch tab and head to the library to pay for a student's lost book. They do it for the kids.

Whenever I've been involved in school or district programs like "Back-to-School Backpacks," "Thanksgiving Food Baskets," and "Adopt a Family for Christmas," the majority of the people doing the giving have always been the schools' own staff members.

One time I was on a phone call with a parent, speaking with him about his son's behavior in class. He said his son might be acting out because he knows they're not going to have Christmas this year. He told me he had a serious back injury and couldn't work. Consequently, no Christmas presents. I asked him what his three kids wanted or needed, and he was pretty quick to supply a list.

After school I stopped at a mall and bought the items the dad suggested, wrapped them at home, and brought them to school the next day. The dad picked them up himself—jumping out of the car he'd left double parked in front of the school, running into the building, and easily bending over and picking up all four big bags of presents at once. While I watched him from the main office's window as he jogged back to his car, I asked the secretary what she knew about him.

"Well, I know he doesn't have a back injury," she said laughing at me.

Apparently, he'd pulled the same scam on another staff member the year prior. While driving home, I kept thinking about what happened. I was angry. I was angry because he lied to me and angry because I had been duped. Mostly, I realized, I was angry because I felt robbed of the good feelings I experienced while buying and wrapping the presents.

The next day I asked the secretary if he could afford to buy his kids Christmas presents. She said she really doubted it. His personal circumstances were pretty bleak.

When school resumed in January, I phoned the dad and asked how Christmas went. The kids, he said, loved their presents. I told him that was good because I planned to buy presents for them again next Christmas. I said I was letting him know now so there'd be no reason for him to worry the kids about not having Christmas presents or any reason for him to lie in order to get help.

At the beginning of December, he called with a list. I told him to scratch off the big bag of M&Ms and the Silly Putty because I thought he'd be able could buy those. I asked him to bring them to me in the next couple of days so I could wrap them and put them with the other gifts—and, he did!

A little boy was seated in the office. When the staff assistant who worked in our computer lab walked in, the boy excitedly announced, "Hey, I know her! She's the lady that lives in the computer land."

CHAPTER TWENTY

"Call Me Maybe"

I N ONE OF MY COLLEGE CLASSES, YEARS AGO, THE PROFESSOR engaged us in a discussion regarding the following two statements:

1) The district office exists to serve the schools.
2) The schools exist to serve the district office.

At that time, as an undergraduate student, I said "The first statement is true—of course." Now, as an experienced, retired principal, I would say, "It depends entirely on the district."

Districts operate very differently from one another. Some operate using a top-down approach wherein power, authority, and decision-making are driven by the organizational chart. Some districts (to varying degrees) operate from an ideology of site-based management and shared decision-making, wherein stakeholders are actively, and genuinely, included. Still others operate in a model wherein one's authority is equal to his or her level of responsibility.

If in all three of these models (authoritarian, shared decision-making, and role authority) a leader at the district office received a serious complaint phone call about one of its schools, this is what might be said to the principal:

1) **Authoritarian**: "Call him back right away. Say this
   _____. Then, call me back to let me know it's done.
   In fact, send me an email, too, so I can have it on file."

2) **Site-based Shared Decision-making**: "Just pull a team
   together to brainstorm solutions. You might consider
   inviting the parent, too, when you get to the decision-making point."

3) **Role Authority**: "Hey, it's your building. Just let me know
   if I can help in any way."

I've worked under all three models. My favorite, by far, was role authority—"Hey, it's your building. Just let me know if I can help in any way." (That, by the way, is an actual quote from a particular central office). In this district, if a problem was called to the attention of any district personnel, they'd simply relay the caller's name and phone number back to the principal.

In the role authority district, central office personnel spent a good portion of their time in the schools, actively engaged in assisting. For example, they were dispersed to buildings to help administer beginning-of-the-year reading assessments. Principals could call upon the district's curriculum department to provide personnel to conduct mini trainings for teachers in their buildings. As much as possible central office personnel would be at their assigned (or selected) school to help the staff and students when it was most needed and greatly appreciated—first day of school, track and field day, picture day, parent's day, graduation day, last day of school, etc.

I absolutely worked my heart out in that "role authority" district. I had such a strong sense of ownership. My building felt like it was my shop and I was 100% personally and professionally invested in student and staff success. I didn't make any daily or long-range decisions based upon wanting to please or placate a supervisor or superintendent but, instead, based solely upon what I knew to be best for students.

In a shared decision-making or site-based management model, it's crucial that it be authentic. I remember telling my daughter she could choose what to wear when she was in elementary school; then, I'd lay out two outfits on top of her bed. That's not authentic. I was running the show. Some organizations do this. They put together teams—say, to write annual school goals—and, they hand pick a parent or two to serve on the committee.

Or, the district claims to be site-based wherein each building has a say in defining and designing its path to success. Then, when the building's staff wants to try something new or research a different strategies, they are told, "No." I have worked in Site-based Shared-Decision-making organizations. The idea was great; the implementation was slow as we were growing into the ideology itself, as much as the practice.

In my experience working within a top-down model it seemed that an element of fear traveled up and down the organizational ladder. Influential parent groups, strong unions, etc. could wield a great deal of power over the organization if they made the organization fear losing control. Employees feared having a complaint call made to supervisors or to the district office. Calls were viewed negatively because no one in the organization wanted the complaint or problem to keep traveling up the chain of command. When I worked in this type of organizational model, I felt it systemically stifled our creativity as a school and as an organization and greatly undermined authority at the classroom, building, and department levels. Responsibility, without authority, feels like what I imagine it would have been like to be a housewife in the 1930's.

Just my opinion.

In my experiences as a principal, issues or problems that happened in my school were resolved in my school. Despite having worked in multiple schools and districts, I can count on just one hand the number of complaint phone calls that went to the central offices. Two that come to mind are "Timmy, the coat man" and "scary Sherry."

"Timmy, the coat man" lived in an apartment complex within walking distance from the school. He appeared on campus one day and collected an armful of coats students had left on the playground after first recess. When a staff member spotted him, he told her he was going to bring them to the office. We explained to Timmy that the kids get hot while playing and leave their coats next to their classroom exterior doors. They will either get them during the next recess or when they exit that door at the end of the day. It's best to just leave them there. We also assured him that any still remaining outside at the end of the day were retrieved and brought into the office.

Apparently, that didn't satisfy him because over and over he tried to come on campus and do the same thing, and over and over we explained why he couldn't be on campus and couldn't collect the children's coats.

One afternoon we got a call from the superintendent's office. Timmy had walked to the superintendent's office and asked what he needed to do to apply for the job of being "the coat man." The superintendent asked if we couldn't find something for him to do as a volunteer.

The next day, when he was on campus, I helped him fill out a volunteer clearance form. The form was returned a few days later. Do to what was on his record, he couldn't volunteer in a school. Although he refused to follow rules, I actually think his heart was in the right place.

Once Timmy got word that he couldn't be a school volunteer, we never saw him again. However, the superintendent's secretary called a couple of months later to share with us that somehow Timmy found out it was the superintendent's birthday and he hand-delivered a birthday card. The front of the card read, "I wish you a Happy Birthday, with all of my *butt*." Inside it read, "I would have said *heart*, but my butt is bigger."

The main office had been closed for well over an hour and I was in my office working on a budget that I really wanted to finish. I didn't want to answer the phone but I did.

It was the district's front office calling. The receptionist had just received a frantic phone call from one of our parents. She knew this parent well from other encounters over the years and knew that when she got angry, she ran very hot. Wasn't news to me. Her youngest children were at my school because she'd threatened to beat up the principal at her children's neighborhood school. She also had an active restraining order to stay off our campus because during open house she'd pushed one of her kid's teacher up against a wall and threatened to beat her up.

According to the receptionist, the parent was furious because her child's kindergarten teacher asked the kids to bring a banana to school the next day, and she didn't have any and didn't want to go to the store.

I knew the kindergarteners were going to be wearing *bandanas* during our school's music performance the following day. The teacher most likely asked students to bring a bandana from home—if they had one. Bandana, not banana. We had a good laugh and the receptionist asked if I would be willing to give the parent a call back.

"Coward," I teased, assuring her that, of course, I'd call "scary Sherry" back.

I asked a first grader to wait in a chair in the office and let me know when he was ready to speak with me about what had happened. After a few minutes he called out "Mrs. President, I'm ready to talk now!"

CHAPTER TWENTY-ONE

"Disco Fever"

AT THREE DIFFERENT SCHOOLS, WE WELCOMED OUR students to the school day with music. After the first bell rang, age-appropriate music would play over the intercom system, throughout the building and on the playgrounds, until the tardy bell sounded. I also loved using music to signal the start of staff meetings or to play at dismissals before breaks.

Black-Eyed Peas' "Let's Get It Started" was a favorite to announce the start of staff meetings. For a couple of years at dismissal before winter break, I dedicated "Hallelujah" to all of our hardworking staff members and volunteers. One year I played "I'm Going Home" and another year, "It's a Wonderful World." At dismissal on the last day of school, the favorite was always "Sha-na-na-na" by the Rubettes.

One time, during a non-student-attendance teacher workday, I played "A Fifth of Beethoven" from "Saturday Night Fever" movie soundtrack—full blast—to signal the beginning of the staff training.

After less than a minute of play, a man came running into the office with his arms flailing about yelling, "Turn it off! Turn it off! Turn it off!"

Turns out, the blaring song interrupted our district superintendent who was, at the time, addressing all of the district's custodians from our school's stage. Oops!

I emailed the superintendent later that day.

"Sincere apologies for this morning's rude disruption. What can I say? Gotta love disco."

His email response: "Much prefer rock 'n' roll!"

The superintendent was in my office a few days later. He was making the rounds to all schools asking each principal for his or her ideas about how we could tighten the district budget. My suggestion was to close the warehouse and order paper and supplies from office supply stores—free next-day delivery and no employee costs.

When I sensed he was getting ready to wrap up his visit, I asked him if he'd be up for pulling a little prank on one of the principals during the next Tuesday meeting. This superintendent had a great sense of humor and I was pretty sure he'd agree.

"Absolutely!" he said without hesitation and with a big grin.

I told him that one particular principal was notorious in our group for forgetting to turn his cell phone off prior to the start of meetings.

He asked who, and then, upon hearing his name, laughed and said, "Oh, this is going to be fun."

The next week, Tuesday's meeting was about halfway over when the superintendent stepped up to the podium. He began speaking to the group about our financial issues and sharing some of the ideas that had been floated by principals regarding ways to tighten the district's budget.

When his cell phone rang loudly, he feigned being mildly annoyed by the interruption while taking his phone from out of his pocket.

"Hello," he said, momentarily covering the mouthpiece with his fingers and mouthing "I'm sorry" to the group.

He spoke into the phone sounding a bit confused, "Hello. What? What was that? Who? Who are you calling for? Well, this is highly unusual, but okay."

Holding the phone out at arm's length, with a puzzled look on his face, he said, "Jim, it's—it's for you."

The principals, including the one being pranked, burst into laughter.

(True story—except for the principal's name.)

A woman from human resources stepped to the front of the meeting room to remind principals that this coming Friday we were again needed to conduct teacher interviews. In this particular district each candidate was interviewed by teams of two principals.

It was actually a pleasant duty. We met idealistic, starry-eyed young people fresh from their student teaching gigs and a few veteran teachers who were reentering the workforce or who had recently moved into the area.

The district did a great job lining up viable candidates for in-district interviews. Seldom did we find candidates sitting across the table from us who were less than stellar.

I always had a soft spot for first-year teachers. They were usually both excited and terrified at the same time. Imagine the level of responsibility they were taking on and, in most cases, were in their early twenties. Just a short time prior they were going to prom and now they're responsible for teaching young minds and conducting parent–teacher conferences.

One first-year gal walked into my office all excited. She'd been busy all day setting up her new classroom and was anxious for me to see the outcome.

"Look, all the chairs match now," she said.

"I traded with other classrooms."

"It's beautiful and I sure understand and appreciate your enthusiasm," I said. "But you're going to need to put all the chairs back," I told her, explaining how other teachers would feel about their chairs being swapped out.

The school year had just begun when a first-year teacher came into my office telling me she had a minor car accident on the way home the day prior. She was rear-ended but the driver was uninsured. I told her that her insurance would likely pay. The next morning she couldn't wait to tell me she had five-hundred dollar deductible.

"That means they're going to pay me five hundred dollars—right?" she asked with a big grin on her pretty face.

This same teacher wanted to speak with me privately a few weeks later. Once we were inside my office she shared that she was pregnant. But, she was concerned about what her students' parents would think because she and her boyfriend weren't married and her title was Miss.

"Well, it doesn't matter what anyone thinks," I told her, "because your family is none of their family's business."

I congratulated her and hugged her.

"Oh, thank you," she said with tears in her pretty blue eyes. "My mom is so far away and I just really needed a mom hug today."

One morning I was told by our office clerk that one of our first-year teachers was devastated because his girlfriend had broken up with him the night before. I went into his classroom before students arrived to make sure he was okay. He melted into a lengthy hug during which he sobbed on my shoulder.

I think I saw my own daughter in these young first-year staffers and, for that reason, wanted to give them extra care and guidance.

It's important for all staff to have friends at work. It's like the old soap opera's opening told us: these are the days of our lives. How sad it would be to work in a place where you had no friends, no support, and no one who cared whether you were there or not.

At one school, when two male staff assistants became friends, I made sure that every school year they were scheduled to have the same lunch period. Both were very intelligent gentlemen. I loved when I would occasionally pop into the staff room when it was their lunch period. They'd be sitting in the overstuffed furniture discussing any number of subjects from history to music to travel.

One year, while making out schedules, I decided our most senior staff assistant should be honored by having her own desk. The custodian moved an extra desk into the computer lab. I asked her to be in charge of safety patrol. Her schedule included a 30-minute period each day during which she worked on safety patrol selections, issues, and scheduling at her desk. She and the computer lab tech became life-long friends.

I think we should honor our most senior classified and certified staff members. Kind of like the military's "twilight tour,"—wherein the last couple of years of service are kinder, gentler.

There's a position that's neither posted nor interviewed for—because it doesn't exist in schools. But, in a perfect world, it would. Nike knows it. Starbucks gets it. Costco recognizes it. That shop in Seattle's Pikes Place Market, where they toss fish to customers, understands it so well they wrote a book.

Businesses and organizations wherein workers feel valued and appreciated, where they have friends, and where they laugh and have fun, are businesses and organizations that retain staff. Teams can't be built where workers come and go—or where leaders come and go. Effective teams are built through shared experiences over time.

The affective domain needs to be addressed. Wouldn't it be wonderful if this were recognized as a valid need and someone was assigned duties such as team building, events planning, and morale maintenance? It would need to be a person who understood the demands of staff at given points throughout the year and would plan accordingly. He or she would keep watch over the pulse of staff morale, and monitor group energy, and serve as a navigator for anyone feeling disconnected.

Staffs need to be more than trained, monitored, and evaluated; they also need to be nurtured. Today's educators often feel overwhelmed and undervalued. Negative media stories, unfunded mandates, escalating student behaviors, fear for personal safety, increasing district demands—these things and more make them wonder if they chose the right career path.

For most, I really don't think the path is wrong. It's just that it's such a damn long and winding path—fraught with steep hills, detours and ruts. They need someone on staff who is responsible for pointing out the flowers along the path (and, when necessary) planting them.

This new position would help to ensure employees could meet their basic needs for fun, freedom, belonging, and recognition in their workplace. Not sure what the position might be called—half-time cheerleader and half-time social director? Or, maybe, "Julie on the Lido Deck?"

Most importantly, educators need everybody from the government on down to the district to step back and take a breath. Quit adding new initiatives, new curricula, additional assessments, more requirements, etc.; instead, start subtracting.

Educators were already stretched to the max before COVID. School closures, online schools and hybrid schools have provided this window of opportunity to rethink what schools should and could look like.

Maybe cut the school day by a couple of hours. Maybe cut the week down to four student attendance days (without adding a single mandatory training or meeting on that fifth day). If teachers and staff assistants could plan together every Wednesday, for example, imagine what could be accomplished. Imagine! If we continue to do what we've always done, we'll continue to get what we've always gotten. If public schools adhere to the same hours and the same yearly schedule—not because it would yield the best results, but, simply, to accommodate parents' work schedules—then, maybe, the best we should hope to be is a first-class child care service.

Just my opinion.

I entered one of our first-grade classrooms along with a visiting school board member. A little boy jumped up from his seat, threw his arms around my waist, and yelled, "It's Mrs. Leary, Praise the Lord!"

CHAPTER TWENTY-TWO

"I Heard it through the Grapevine"

A SCHOOL IS KIND OF LIKE A SMALL TOWN. JUST AS IN any town the people in it experience illnesses, deaths, marriages, births, divorces. Such is life.

At one of my schools, when two staff members became involved and the spouse of one of them was also on staff, it made for some pretty out-of-control gossip. The tension was palpable and staff morale was suffering.

As an administrator I had never dealt with this before, but my intuition was telling me to do something. When drama inside the school reached a point at which talk in the hallways became whispered and rooms fell silent when someone entered, I felt it was time to clear the air. Gossip and taking sides is toxic to the spirit of being a team.

I asked each of the three persons (individually) if they trusted me enough to allow me to speak with staff. I told them I believed it was necessary to help everyone move past this. All three agreed. I also asked that they not be present. They agreed to that condition, as well.

We held the all-staff meeting in a classroom so the door could be closed and no non-staff person could overhear. I was the only one who spoke. I was very frank and told them up front that I would not answer any questions after.

I named the individuals and said, "You may have heard that Person A is in a relationship with Person C. I have their permission to confirm this. You may have also heard that Person B is angry and made very serious accusations about Person A, which were later recanted. I have their permission to confirm this.

Bottom line, if only one of these individuals worked at this school—any one of the three—then, all of their personal lives could play themselves out and we wouldn't know a thing, unless they wanted us to know. But, because all three work here, it feels as though we have front-row seats to their story. Remember, it is their story and as such, it's not ours to tell. If we're not talking about it, the whispers in the halls will end. If we're not talking about it, rooms won't fall silent when someone else enters.

It's not a made-for-TV drama or a daytime soap opera; it's people's lives. They deserve to be able to live their lives without our judgment or interference.

Each of these individuals plays an important role on our staff, and my expectation is that we all will continue to respect their expertise and access their services for our students.

In the days, weeks, and months ahead, let's please give each of these three people an equal measure of privacy and kindness."

No one said a word when I left the room and it was still silent by the time I reached the hallway doors. Staff members began leaving the room—one after another—and, still, no one was talking.

I was immediately second-guessing my "clear the air" intuition. Had I made a terrible error in judgement and made things even worse?

By the time I got back to my office and turned on my computer, there were five emails thanking me for the meeting. One staff member said it feels like we've "opened a festering wound and it's already beginning to heal."

A kindergartner spoke up during a classroom lesson about seasons,
"Teacher, I already learned all about Autumn and Eve at my church."

CHAPTER
TWENTY-THREE

"Candle in the Wind"

SEPTEMBER 11, 2001 WAS A TUESDAY. WE PRINCIPALS were on the road, headed to our district's regularly-scheduled meeting, where several district personnel were waiting curbside to tell each arriving principal that the meeting was cancelled and why. I turned into the parking lot just as my husband was leaving. He motioned for me to pull alongside his car and we both rolled our windows down.

"You have to go back to your school right away," he told me. "The meeting's been cancelled. Turn on your radio."

I made a quick U-turn in the parking lot and headed off for my building, fiddling with the radio dial to find out what was going on. As it happened, my car's radio had been malfunctioning. It would work for a minute or two, start crackling, and then go quiet. I'd have to turn it off and back on again, and within a couple of minutes the cycle would repeat. We'd been meaning to take the car in to get it fixed. Really wishing we had.

I was desperately trying to hear what was going on, but it wasn't making sense. Newscaster Peter Jennings was talking about a commercial airliner crashing into the tower. I remember thinking, "Why is Peter Jennings reporting about my school; and, what tower is he talking about?"

When my husband said, "You have to get back to your school," I personalized what he was saying and assumed something terrible had happened specifically at my school.

Arriving on campus, I ran into the staff room, where five people stood spellbound watching the television. Everyone was silent. What was unfolding was horrendous. I just wanted to go home, gather my family safely around me, and mourn the loss of lives and our innocence. As a nation I don't think many of us could have ever imagined such invasive evil. When the aircraft breached the Pentagon, I felt physically ill. I had worked there for three years when I was in the Navy and had such fond memories of and great respect for that building and its forty thousand workers.

There was no time for personal reflection or grief. By then, teachers were arriving, and school would begin in less than an hour. Time to shift gears into principal mode and foresee all the ways this could impact staff and students today.

I held an emergency before-school staff meeting during which we had a moment of silence for those who lost lives, for their loved ones, and for the emergency responders who were risking their own lives.

"Some of you might have family or friends who work in the towers or in the Pentagon or, you might have a loved one scheduled to fly today," I said, acknowledging that some staff members might be very personally touched by what was unfolding.

"If you have a personal connection and need to leave for the day, let me know and we will secure a substitute for you," I assured them.

Sometimes, when a significant tragedy occurs, we can become overwhelmed with emotion even when there is no connection other than we are witnessing a very raw and human experience.

"If, for any reason, you feel unsteady or overwhelmed today and need to step away from your class or duty for a moment, please call the office. We will take care of you."

I asked that no one turn on a classroom television or radio and that they make certain students kept cell phones turned off and put away. I also asked staff members to avoid engaging in conversation with students even if a student asks questions about the attacks. The best response would be something along the lines of, "We really don't know much right now; hopefully we will all know more at the end of the day. If you have any questions, ask your parents."

On that day absenteeism was slightly higher than usual. I suspect parents had the same feeling I did about keeping loved ones close. After I went to my office, I called my husband just to hear his voice.

Less than a month after September 11th I was scheduled to fly across country to attend a national educator's conference on the topic of English as a Second Language. I called the gentleman in charge of the ESL program for the district. I told him my daughter was afraid for me to travel and, if possible, I'd like to skip the conference. He was both gracious and understanding. Confession: I lied. I was afraid. Of course, I've flown many times and many miles since that tragic day but, air travel just a month after watching the towers tumble was way too soon.

On the day of the tragic Sandy Hook shootings, I felt it was necessary to go to every classroom to tell every teacher. That same afternoon several parent volunteers were scheduled to be in classrooms to help kids decorate the gingerbread houses they'd made. My worry was twofold: teachers could be caught off guard by a parent telling them about the news and, students could overhear conversations between parents and teachers. Having advance knowledge about it they'd be better able to keep emotions in check and to quickly cut off any conversation initiated by parents that could be overheard by students.

Once I opened a classroom door, I stood in the doorway and motioned for the teacher to step outside the classroom. Each very short briefing began with "Something has happened, and it has nothing to do with your family." I told them about the shootings and that the situation was still active. Then I explained my concern about talk between parents and staff that could be overheard by students. When I finished making rounds, I sent an email to all staff to make sure everyone was in the loop.

On three separate occasions I needed to tell my staff that one of our own had passed. Twice the announcement was not unexpected. Early in the year, our computer teacher was told the lung cancer for which she had been receiving aggressive treatment had metastasized to her brain. She decided to stay home and forego further treatment.

The principal asked me (his associate principal) to cover two wings of our building and he would cover the other two. He wanted us to move quickly through the building, calling staff members to the door and whispering to them in the hall that Ms. Charles had passed. He wanted to make sure no one would feel slighted having heard second hand or having heard later than others. We never really know who is close to whom. We just see the trees. We don't see the roots.

Ms. Charles was the woman who advised me to never have a meeting when I can send an email, to never send an email if I can slip a note in her box and, to never put a note in her box if I can just tell her in the hall.

Ironically, here we were—just a few months after that conversation—sharing news of her passing by telling staff members in the hall. Somehow, I think she would have been okay with that.

The second time it was a primary-level teacher who also had cancer. She taught the year prior—taking a day here and a day there, whenever her most recent blood draw showed her white blood cell count was up and her immunity was down. I informed everyone during a staff meeting the morning after she passed. Many who were close to her already knew.

At another school, a staff assistant went to the hospital with a horrible headache. She'd been suffering severe headaches for some time and ended up being admitted to the hospital. Our school's nurse called me at home that same evening. I remember she asked me to sit down and then told me the young woman was brain dead. It's strange how you can clearly hear something but, at the same time, not clearly understand.

I recall saying something like, "But, she'll be okay, right?"

The next morning during an all-staff meeting, I informed everyone about her unexpected passing. I'll never forget the sound of that collective gasp in the room. She worked in a special education class and also worked in our "solutions room"—helping kids solve problems that arose during recesses. Consequently, she was known by a large percentage of our students. The school district did a wonderful job providing on-site counselors to help both students and staff deal with the news and the loss.

We were unclear about what was wrong with her and the circumstances surrounding her death in the hospital. But, as I would have expected, the staff rallied—providing all the food and flowers for her memorial service.

She loved sunflowers. Long after her passing, sunflowers would appear at school—a sweet vaseful on the office counter, a large sunflower topping the Christmas tree in the staff room.

Three times in my career I facilitated a staff member being told of the passing of a loved one. Each time I walked into the teacher's classroom and asked him or her to come with me; and each time the person suspected it was not for a good reason because I arrived with a staff member to take over the class. There is no easy way to do this.

A third-grade teacher, who is very close to his wonderful family, received a call during the school day from his wife to let him know that his father had just died.

A kindergarten teacher's father died right about the time his wife was due to deliver their first child. So, of course, when I entered the room, he flashed a big grin expecting good news. I very quickly told him his wife wasn't in labor and she was fine but needed to speak with him.

The third was a call from the police informing a teacher that her husband had been killed at the scene when a car hit him while he was riding his bicycle.

These calls are devastating for the individuals, so the last thing anyone would want would be for them to take that call in a room or office they would have to go into again. I chose a small auxiliary office, the custodian's office, even the electrical room—wherever there was a phone that the call could be transferred to in a place the person could always avoid.

When a rock-steady reliable teacher didn't show up for work one day, it was very concerning. I called her home and she seemed disoriented. Her husband took her to the hospital right away where it was discovered that she had a staph infection on her spine. She underwent emergency surgery, followed by an extended stay in the hospital during which she had two additional surgeries. Once she was released from the hospital, she spent a lengthy period of time in rehabilitation. For several weeks, I met regularly with the staff, providing updates on her condition. Behind the scenes, I met regularly with a particular staff member to pray for our colleague's healing. Separation of church and state has nothing to do with silent or private prayer in school. In every school I'd worked in, I was blessed to have connected with a prayer partner. I was even blessed to be part of a small cadre of principals who welcomed the opportunity to pray for one another's school, students, and staff.

A teacher had been experiencing headaches and was becoming forgetful, so he made an appointment to find out the cause. He had a brain tumor. He immediately underwent surgery, followed by treatment. He was a beloved colleague and friend. Staff members were heartbroken to see him in pain and joined in with an army of family and friends, cheering on his courage and determination. He and his family modeled living every last moment to its fullest—going on trips and spending every minute with loved ones. After he passed, a huge building at the county fairgrounds was the only venue large enough to accommodate the number of people wanting to celebrate this young man's life and honor his family.

It was mid-August when my best friend died. She was on a girls' trip in central Oregon when she suffered an asthma episode. In the middle of the night, she was found clutching her inhaler and gasping for air at the top of the stairs in their resort condo. Her sister and the friends she was with called 911. She died onboard Life Flight before it reached the hospital.

This loss hit me very hard. Not only had she been my best friend for many, many years but she was also the school clerk at one of my schools and had transferred to become the school secretary at two subsequent schools where I served as principal.

At her funeral I saw a parent who had been repeatedly demanding and unkind to her. The first thing that ran through my mind was that I couldn't wait to call my best friend to tell her who was at her funeral. I wanted to call her every day. Every day I had a question for her or a funny story to share or I wanted to tell her something about my daughter or grandchildren. I lost my closest friend, and, ironically, the thing I needed most was to talk about it with my closest friend.

When principals' pre-duty days began, I was in my office preparing for the opening of the school year. The building was eerily silent and out of the blue I started crying and just could not stop. Within the hour all principals were expected to meet at a luncheon across town to welcome new staff members. I'd tried splashing water on my face and turning on upbeat music. Nothing was working. I wasn't even sure I could drive safely.

Getting ready for school's opening without my sidekick and partner in crime was heartbreaking, and the resultant tears didn't trickle—they steadily streamed.

I called my supervisor's office. Her secretary could not have been kinder. She told me to hang up and just wait there. Her words were sweetly soothing.

"Don't you go anywhere, sweet pea. Do you hear me?" she said in the most loving tone. "You don't even worry about that silly luncheon. You just stay right there."

Within about fifteen minutes, from my office window, I saw my supervisor (and friend) pulling into the school's parking lot. I walked outside to meet her and we sat on a bench together in the warm sun. She told me that in her experiences with grief it had been like this for her, as well; it came in waves—sneaking up, grabbing hold, not letting go—sometimes when it was least expected.

When my husband's car pulled into the parking lot, she told me she hoped I didn't mind that she'd made an executive decision to call him. She told us to go for a drive, go have a nice lunch together, and go home.

During Tuesday's meeting's break, I was approached by the principal of the school my friend had been working at when she passed. He said he knew we were close and he was so sorry. He shared that in the short time she'd been at his school, she completely changed the tenor for the better. He asked if I would mind packing her desk and taking her belongings to her husband. He said it felt more appropriate for me to do it than him. I told him I'd be honored to do this for her.

The following day, while cleaning out her desk drawers I felt a soft pat on my shoulder. The custodian who'd worked at my school for only a short time, while awaiting placement in this middle school assignment—the one whose work ethic reminded me of my father's—was standing behind me. After a hug he told me how much he was going to miss my friend. She was so loved.

Sorting through her desk I ran across cards I'd given to her over the years all bundled together and neatly tied with a red ribbon. She had also saved dozens and dozens of thank-you cards and notes from staff members and parents—"Thank you for attending my son's graduation"; "Thank you for coming to my son's Boy Scout ceremony"; "Thank you for bringing treats for my class"; "Thank you for giving my husband and I a night away at the coast"; "Thank you for cheering us on at the soccer game"; "Thank you for bringing coffee cake for the staff room"; "Thank you for coming to our daughter's baptism." Thank you, thank you, thank you, thank you…

Throughout her life she was an exemplar of service to others. For me, she was the sister I never had, the mother I yearned for, and the best friend of a lifetime.

For the first few days after her passing, I was experiencing a very unexpected emotion—jealousy. So many women were talking about and posting that she was their best friend. That couldn't be. She was MY best friend. When the dust settled and reason ruled again, I realized so many of us identified this woman as being OUR best friend; yet, not one of us really knew who was HER best friend.

Who among us wouldn't want that to be their legacy?

The six-year-old Pacific Islander who wasn't accustomed to wearing shoes hopped his way down the hall to the office at least once a day saying, "Hot feet! Hot feet!" Whoever was available would take his shoes off, give him a cool cloth to put on his feet, and then lace him up and send him back to class.

CHAPTER TWENTY-FOUR

"Oops! I Did It Again"

I MAGINE MY SHOCK WHEN I WALKED BY A CLASSROOM AND peeking inside the open door, saw a braided noose suspended from the ceiling! The teacher—an excellent educator, by the way—provided the visual because it "fit into the current unit of study."

"Take it down, immediately," I whispered at the doorway.

There are some things that are just flat-out inappropriate. Providing a visual of how to braid a noose is one of those things.

Interestingly, the year prior, this same teacher asked me to sign a form to forward to the curriculum department requesting *To Kill a Mockingbird* be added to the list of approved elementary-level books. The teacher wanted to read it aloud to her class. It was a favorite book that she had first read during high school.

"Please repeat what you just said," I said.

"My favorite book from high school," the teacher said—with a knowing nod and a smile after saying the words "high school."

Sometimes even the best teachers, perhaps because they are so passionate about their work, can have a lapse in judgment. For example, the teacher who wanted to take her class kayaking or the teacher who wanted to take his class on a weekend camping trip to the beach. The teacher who arranged for an assembly for her entire grade-level without getting permission from the principal or the teacher who wanted to start a "bee keeping" project on campus. Or, how about the teacher who involved her entire school in a statewide recycling competition and signed a contract to have the money raised from the recycling company donated to the Humane Society—without approval from the either the district or her building principal.

Okay, that last teacher was actually me. We won the competition— but, still.

One of my first duties during my principal's internship was to plan our back-to-school staff get-together. There were no new initiatives or curricula that year, so we could afford ourselves a more relaxing social get-together than usual.

As it happened, I was interning in the same building as another teacher. She graciously volunteered to line up her condominium's community clubhouse for the event. We ran this by the principal and he thought it was a great idea.

When we were talking with him about doing something to inspire and motivate, we asked what he thought of showing the movie *"Teachers"* during lunch. He'd seen the movie on television and gave his approval; so, I rented the VHS video from our local Blockbuster.

As co-interns, we paid for and prepared breakfast trays of assorted pastries, cheeses, and fruit. We filled little bowls with candies and placed them strategically throughout the room.

Everyone entered to the sound of smooth jazz playing softly on a boom box and the smell of freshly-brewed coffee. We spent the morning introducing new staff and going over the nuts and bolts of opening the school year. Staff members signed up for library check-out times and committees on which they were willing to serve.

When lunchtime arrived, so did multiple boxes of pizza. Staff gathered around the television (pre-giant flat screen days), and I popped the video into the machine.

Not too far into the movie our principal walked over, leaned toward the other intern and I, and whispered, "You know, I didn't remember this movie having bad language in it." During the scene in which the movie's principal, Judd Hirsch, gets drunk with his teacher, Nick Nolte, our very conservative, straight-laced principal was pacing around in the small kitchenette area.

When the movie progressed to the scene in which Jobeth Williams walks down the school's hallway naked, our principal's complexion looked even paler than usual. He pulled open the sliding glass door and stepped outside onto the porch. My co-intern and I hurriedly joined him to make sure he was okay.

"This must be a different movie," he said nervously, using his paper napkin to wipe away the glistening beads of sweat that had started collecting above his upper lip. "I've never seen this movie. Is this like a sequel?"

We realized what the problem was. The other intern and I saw the movie at theaters. He'd only seen the edited G-rated version that aired on television—sans explicit language, drinking, and nudity. He was, in a way, correct; they were two completely different movies.

We assured him we would explain to the staff that he'd seen the unedited theater version and would have never approved this version of the movie.

"Yes, please," he said, without hesitation, "please do that."

Everyone makes mistakes and I sure made my fair share. When I had my first building, I made a glaring spelling error on the first staff bulletin. I didn't make the mistake once; I made it five times! It was almost as if my old third-grade nemesis (spelling) had come back to haunt me.

*Teachers: Please check today's rooster against your class list. If a
student's name is not on your class list but appears on today's
rooster put a check mark next to the name on the rooster. Be sure to
return your rooster to the office by 9 AM. You will receive a new
rooster tomorrow.*

Lots and lots of teasing! I'd hear a rooster call or two when I'd walk
by the staff room and, for days, stuffed toy roosters were left on my desk
and in my mailbox. This wasn't a bad thing though. It sure broke the ice,
gave us all something to laugh about and, right off the bat, the staff was
able to see how I handled being wrong and being teased.

A parent came into the office and dropped a paper bag onto the
counter. Before turning to leave, he mentioned the contents were snacks
for his son's class—peanut butter and crackers. "Wait a minute," the
secretary called out, "Remember, some kids have peanut allergies. We
can't give them peanuts."

"I thought of that," he responded. "That's why I didn't buy crunchy."

A fifth-grade teacher sent a student to the office with a note that
read, "Nolan needs to be out of class during our party due to misbehavior.
Can he stay with you for the next thirty minutes?"

Much as I personally didn't like taking away class parties, field
trips, and such, for behaviors, I folded the note and told the boy to take
a seat in one of the chairs in the hallway just outside of my office. I told
him he could choose a book from the bottom shelf of my bookcase to
take with him. He chose *James and the Giant Peach* and obediently took
a seat. I set the timer on my desk and returned to writing my parent
newsletter article.

The timer's alarm was going to ring in about five minutes, so I
turned it off and called for the student.

"Nolan?"

When he didn't respond, I assumed he might have fallen asleep.

"Nolan?" I called out a little louder, again receiving no response.

I walked into the hall where I discovered him wide awake and still silently reading.

"Nolan, why didn't you answer me?" I asked.

"My name's Chris," the boy responded politely.

Chris was just delivering the note. In the meantime, Nolan was still back in the classroom and the teacher had been so busy with the class celebration she didn't realize Chris hadn't returned and Nolan hadn't left.

I apologized to Chris and called his mother to let her know what happened. She told me the kids were celebrating that everyone in the class had completed reading ten library books. What they had chosen for their celebration was donuts and silent reading.

Thankfully he'd been reading the whole time and the next day I brought two Krispy Kreme donuts to school for him.

When two cars collided in our parking lot just before school, I wasn't too happy when I found out the associate principal didn't immediately radio me. Our clerk happened to look out the window, and when she realized there'd been a fender bender, she knocked on the conference room door to get me out of a meeting.

When I arrived at the scene, the assistant principal had just finished putting a spare tire on the front of a woman's car. I walked to the other side of her car and then motioned for him to come around. The rear tire on that side was also completely flat.

I asked him to stand by the entrance to the school, stop every car, and let the parents know that it was just a fender bender, that no one was hurt, and to drive slowly around the two cars.

Lesson learned: Make sure to gather all information before acting.

Returning from carpool duty after dismissal, I noticed two beautiful little girls seated in the office because they had missed the bus. I asked the attendance clerk to get the parents on the phone. She told me they didn't speak English but I said to call anyway and I'd try my best. Once the mom was on the phone, I accessed my very limited amount of Spanish.

"Buenos tardes. Tus hijos estan en la esquela," I said.

The woman said several words—none of which I understood.

"Soy la directora, Senora Leary, y tus hijos estan en la esquela," I repeated.

Her next three or four sentences were completely lost on me and I remember thinking—what are the chances I wouldn't know even a single word she was saying?

"What are you doing?" the clerk said, taking the receiver from me.

"They're Somalian."

Lesson learned: Don't make assumptions.

A little boy was supposed to be picked up by his father after school. It was 4:00 P.M. and then 5:00 P.M. Something was wrong. No one was answering at his home. At 6:00 P.M. I called the police and asked them to go to the home to do a welfare check. Then, I took the little boy into the school's kitchen and put together a few things for him to eat. The police showed up after 7:00 P.M. with the boy's father in tow.

When they checked on the house, a neighbor saw them and said that the man went fishing. Thankfully, he knew the area where he most often fished. The police located him standing in the water, absolutely exhausted.

He had waded out just far enough that he became stuck thigh-level in the muddy river bed. His legs had been sucked into the thick mud and he couldn't free himself. He knew not to struggle because he could be pulled in farther, so when he tired of standing, he just leaned backward and allowed the top portion of his body to float in the water. He had been there for hours. No one could see him from the road and, when he yelled at passing cars, no one could hear him. By the time the police found him his legs were cramping terribly. Thankfully it was late enough in the year that both the air and the shallow water were warm. I always felt horrible that I didn't call the police earlier.

Lesson learned: Don't hesitate to call for help right away.

You wouldn't think it would be difficult to choose programs for student assemblies. But choosing assemblies that are entertaining, educational, and appropriate for grades K-5? That's difficult. For a couple of years I delegated this duty to the associate principal. My only two caveats were involve some teachers in the choosing, and do not schedule the snake man (personal phobia).

One assembly we had was a life-size puppet show wherein elaborate puppet costumes were worn by dancers and performers. At the start of the performance, a man wearing a very convincing giant lizard costume (with green, glowing eyes) clawed his way across the stage and then pretended he was going to slither down the apron of the stage right in front of where our kindergarten students were seated on the floor. There was no way this was going to end well.

Students take their cues from the adults they trust. We were pretty much in a holding pattern until a teary-eyed little girl looked up at her teacher. The first-year teacher, wanting to soothe her student, jumped out of her chair, hurried to the front row where the girl was seated, and cradled the little one in her arms. This signaled to the others: "Yes, you have reason to be afraid."

As our youngest students suddenly stood up, en masse, I ran for the doors that led back into the rest of the school. My standing there trying to block the doorway with both arms outstretched yelling, "It's okay, it's okay," did absolutely nothing. The stampede commenced. Seventy-five screaming five-year-olds, running directly toward me, is something I never want to experience again. I honestly thought they were going to trample me and my demise would be featured on the six o'clock news. Those who shot past me were redirected to the art room where their teachers could pick them up.

I told the assembly company to turn on the lights and get the lizard off the stage immediately.

We reseated about half of the kindergartners—the ones who hadn't made their way out of the gym. The rest of the students stayed in the art room. I think it took two more assemblies before our youngest students trusted that they wouldn't be scared again.

It's not on the Tuesday meeting agenda, but the superintendent steps up to the podium. We weren't accustomed to him doing this often, but, under the circumstances, we weren't surprised. His reason for the drop-in was to remind us to not make any statements to the news reporters.

As he was speaking, news crew vans were stationed in the parking lot and across the street, hoping to get some footage and comments for the nightly news. This morning's newspaper already broke the story—that was being jokingly referred to by some principals as "Watergate."

Using district funds and personnel, the superintendent had a shower built in the restroom adjoining his office. It wasn't pre-approved by the school board, and instantly the "taxpayer expense" and "sense of entitlement" angles became fodder for local reporters. Mistakes are made even at the highest levels.

His rationale for the shower was that he liked to run after work for exercise and needed to be able to shower and change his clothes whenever he had a district meeting or evening event after his run. Also, by having a shower at work, he wouldn't need to be reimbursed for mileage to go to and from home to shower and change.

If they're talking about you or laughing at you, I've always heard wise people say, "might as well join them." Might have been better to come into the meeting wearing a shower cap, with a towel draped over one shoulder, carrying a back scrubber. Could have even had *Sesame Street's* "Rubber Ducky" all cued up for his entrance. That way, we could all have a laugh together.

Then, immediately, own the mistake. No explanations, no excuses—just own it. Reimburse the district for the full cost of the shower and ask for a receipt to deduct the donation on income tax.

Just my opinion.

A fifth grader was in my office for having started a fight. After speaking with him and the other student, I said, "Here's the deal." He covered his ears and started yelling, "No, don't say that! Don't say that!" I asked him what in the world was wrong, and he told me, "Every time you say 'here's the deal,' I end up suspended!"

CHAPTER TWENTY-FIVE

"Let's Misbehave"

MASS MEDIA STORIES ABOUT SCHOOLS ARE SELDOM good. Actually, any news stories are seldom good. The unfortunate thing is that negative reporting results in skewed views. Yes, student behaviors have become more challenging over the years. Yes, there are schools in our country with armed guards and metal detectors, and, yes, it's because there is need for them.

As a principal I have had things thrown at me and been kicked, shoved, punched, bitten and spat upon. But the good news is that these behaviors were far from the norm. They were the exceptions. The vast majority (80-90%) of the students in every school I worked in never saw me for disciplinary reasons.

And the majority of misbehaviors weren't alarming. These are just little kids, after all. They're learning how to manage behaviors—just as they're learning how to read. Part of our job as educators is to help them identify feelings (anger, jealousy, embarrassment, etc.) and to help them learn to choose appropriate and effective responses and behaviors.

In each school, there were some serious behaviors meriting suspension or expulsion. My preferred style, however, was to problem-solve with students and, whenever possible, facilitate opportunities for restitution.

When a student turned the restroom lights out on a much younger student, the two were brought together so the "victim" could share how he felt about what happened. Of course, I asked the little one in advance if he wanted to do this. He was honest and articulate. He said he was really afraid because he thought a bad guy might be in the restroom. He also said now he's a little afraid of the bigger kids at school.

In speaking with the fourth grader, who turned out the lights, I asked him if he would like the opportunity to fix what he had done. He was agreeable and I told him to think of things he might be able to do that would be helpful for the little boy.

That afternoon he came in with his plan. For the balance of the week, he would spend his morning and afternoon recesses on the primary playground. He would play whatever the little boy wanted to play to help him not be afraid of him or other big kids.

In the end, the fourth grader actually took the little one under his wing—even meeting him at his classroom door each day after school and walking him to his bus.

When a girl grabbed another girl on the playground and ripped her blouse, with my sewing kit and a little help, she repaired the blouse. But then she owed me for my time. She suggested her straightening all of the books in my bookshelves and I agreed to her plan.

When we move away from punishment and think of discipline as learning opportunities and teaching students to want to fix or repair what they've done, it's a win-win. The victim feels heard and made whole again, and the misbehaving student learns how his or her behavior impacts others and is able to rectify situations. When we look at a misbehaving child differently we see a different child.

It had been an especially busy morning and I still had three teacher evaluations on my schedule and four bus referrals on my desk. Then, I got a call for "room service."

In several schools I used the code "room service" in lieu of broadcasting to everyone (via walkie--talkies) that a child was out of control and needed to be removed from his or her class. When I entered the room, I discovered two boys needed to go with me to the office. They'd been arguing about whose turn it was on the classroom computer. The teacher said they'd been having trouble getting along and had been arguing a lot lately.

When I got back to the office, I realized the recess bell was going to ring in three minutes. I didn't have time to begin a discussion with the boys because I needed to supervise recess for an absent staff assistant.

I have no idea why this silly idea popped into mind, but I handed the boys a manila envelope and told them to go outside. I told them they couldn't play or talk with anyone else. At the end of recess, they were to bring me back one thousand blades of grass inside the envelope—exactly one thousand—with no roots attached.

When the bell rang, the boys reported back to the office. One of the boys handed me the envelope and told me it had one thousand blades of grass inside.

"Honest," the other boy said, "you can count them."

Then the other child told me, "We know why you made us do that."

Intrigued (since I didn't have an agenda), I said, "Tell me."

"Because we had to work together and we had to depend on each other to keep track of the number. And, when one of us would want to quit, the other would say, 'No, you can do it.'"

I asked how that related to the problems they were having in the classroom. They were quiet for a minute. Then one boy spoke up saying, if we can do something as hard as bending down over and over and picking one thousand blades of grass, then we ought to be able to do something as easy as deciding whose turn it is on the computer.

"Yeah," his buddy chimed in, "teamwork!"

Sagged pants wasn't even an issue 1950's principals ever had to worry about. In many of today's schools, it's a daily occurrence. I always kept curling ribbon on hand just for this problem.

Whenever a boy was sent to the office for wearing sagged pants, I used the ribbon to tighten the waist of his pants. Pulling the back loops together, I'd tie them tightly by knotting a length of ribbon. I'd cut the ends off, being sure to leave some excess hanging. Usually the boy would tell me I left the ends too long. So, I'd assure him I'd take care of that. Then, using my thumb and a single blade of the scissors, I'd make nice tight curls with the excess ribbon.

In every school, there were a few students whose behaviors were outside the norm. Sometimes disciplinary measures had to be taken for more serious offences. Principals' top desk drawers, by year's end, usually had a small assortment of items collected from students—sling shots, bullets, pocket knives, laser pointers.

At a Tuesday meeting, a principal raised his hand and asked the safety director what he suggested we do with these items that had been confiscated from students but not picked up by parents. Someone in the back called out, "Craigslist." Nothing wrong with a little comic relief.

A frantic walkie-talkie call reported that one of our most challenging students was running up the stairs to climb out of a second-story window to go onto the roof. As quickly as I possibly could I ran up the stairs behind him, almost catching up with him in the hallway. Fortunately, I reached the classroom just in time. The student had one leg outside the window and was ready to jump onto the overhang. Grabbing hold of the back of the boy's tee shirt, I twisted it into a tight wad inside my fist. Using the firm hold I had on the shirt, I pulled him back inside the window.

That afternoon, during the weekly staff meeting, a colleague presented me with a handmade certificate reading "First Place to Karen Leary: Fastest 50-yard dash by a Principal in Red High Heels." Thirty-three years later, I still have the certificate and I'm still in touch with the dear friend who made it for me.

A six-year-old was disruptive and violent in the classroom every single day. When the teacher tried to call the office for help one morning, the student ripped the phone from out of the wall. When two staff members were holding the crash bar on a door trying to keep the child from exiting and running, the child bit the forearm of one of the adults. Not just a bitemark but a "rip the skin and underlying tissue gash, with blood everywhere, go get a tetanus shot now" kind of bite. When the child returned to school a couple of days later, the student kicked me in the shin so hard a blood vessel ruptured. I called the appropriate district person to inform her I was emergency expelling the student so we could come up with a plan to protect everyone's safety. Her reaction was, "Oh, Karen, for a little kindergartner?"

The following school year we registered a first-grade student who displayed unimaginable strength whenever he was angry. One time, he ducked under a large round conference table and, with his back, lifted the table legs off of the ground. I pushed the table down and hopped up on it—scooting myself to the middle—thinking adding my weight would stop the student from tipping the table over. The table, to my surprise, continued to move! When this child was in full-on anger mode, it was like witnessing someone who had superhuman strength. The counselor and I were looking for him one day when we finally spotted him stretched, horizontally, between the vertical door jams at the very top of a hallway door's opening. With his hands and feet he had climbed his way horizontally up the doorway—Spiderman style.

One day I arrived on campus to find blue and black graffiti spray painted on one side of the building, and it looked as though the "artist" signed his or her work with initials. The writing looked fairly unsophisticated—not quite up to gang standards. My guess was middle school.

I called the nearest middle school, and, using her computer, the school's clerk looked up students whose first and last names matched the initials I'd provided. The associate principal's intention was to call in each of the six whose initials matched to see if they knew anything about the graffiti. He was able to suspend the search after the second boy he called in had a significant amount of blue and black paint adhering to every cuticle and a fine mist of paint dots on the right sleeve of his jacket. The boy came to see me after school the following day, and we worked together to come up with a form of restitution. He spent the following Saturday (with his parents' permission) weeding our front courtyard.

It was fifth-grade promotion day, and the kids were buzzing with excitement. In the midst of it all, one fifth grader yelled at his teacher, in front of the whole class, "Fuck you!" I called his parents to come and pick him up, as he was suspended for the balance of the day.

When the parents arrived, they said they were shocked that I would do that. It was his special day. How could I take that away from him? Of course, I reminded them that it was his behavior that resulted in him being excluded. They very much wanted to bargain.

"How about he stays today and misses the last day of school tomorrow?" the father asked.

"No," the boy whined. "It's field day tomorrow."

His mother asked if maybe he could miss the first day of middle school next year. I told them we weren't bargaining. What he said to his teacher was inappropriate. When he chose to say it was unfortunate.

They agreed to take him home; but, on their way out, I overheard the boy's mother say, "We'll stop and get you a Dairy Queen ice cream on the way home. Would you like that, honey?"

One morning the school secretary rushed a little boy into my office and handed me his backpack. He had been handing out bullets on the bus. The urgency with which she acted was appropriate. We needed to account for all of the bullets, and, more importantly, we needed to find out if there was a gun. I asked her to call the district office to fill them in on what we were facing. A male staff assistant stayed with the boy in the health room, and his coat and backpack remained in my locked office while I called the police.

Two officers arrived immediately and took responsibility for searching the backpack and coat and the student's pockets. The bus driver had already searched the bus as we'd requested. There was no gun. Inside his backpack, however, the police found a loaded magazine and a box of bullets that appeared to have five missing.

It was easy to retrieve the five missing bullets, thanks to a quick-thinking staff assistant who detained the students who'd ridden on the bus in the school's entryway. We simply asked if anyone was given anything on the bus that morning, we needed them to give it to us. Six students stepped forward and I was handed five bullets and a package of Hostess Twinkies.

The police took the bullets and magazine. They discovered they were from a gun at the child's home that was underneath the father's bed. The gun ended up being identified as stolen.

Whenever something out of the ordinary happens at school, it typically generates the need for a letter to the parents from the principal. This was one of those occasions. All students were given a letter to take home that day.

> *Dear Parents,*
>
> *This morning a student brought bullets to school. All of the bullets were immediately accounted for and police were involved to ensure everyone's safety. There was NO gun. Bullets are not considered a weapon but are an explosive. The student who brought these items to school is facing swift and appropriate consequences.*
>
> *If you have any questions or concerns, do not hesitate to call me.*
>
> *Mrs. Leary, Principal*

One afternoon, right at dismissal time, a teacher called the office to say he'd seen a particular student approaching the playground with a gun. It was the worst possible timing. The dismissal bell had just sounded. Students were exiting all doors. Parents were pulling up in front of the school. Buses were just beginning to load and half of the students were still inside the building and the other half were already outside. Whatever call I made had the potential to become a disaster.

"Dammit, make a call!" I said to myself, silently.

I grabbed the intercom's microphone from off of the counter and switched it on. "Staff and students, secure the building. Staff and students, secure the building."

This was our wording for lockdown (it has since been changed). The few students who had just exited and were still very near the building were scooped inside prior to locking doors.

We called to those on bus duty via radios to let them know we were in lockdown mode and to tell them to load the students as quickly as possible and send the buses away.

The clerk was calling the district office and the secretary was on a call to 911 when a teacher escorted the boy suspected of having a gun to the office. The teacher handed it to me and said it was a pellet gun. Upon hearing that we had both the student and the weapon secured in the office, the police sent officers instead of activating the SWAT team.

So often cameras are at the wrong angle or faces aren't identifiable. In this instance everything lined up. We could clearly see the boy walk onto campus with the pellet gun and aim it at a girl who was standing nearby. We could also clearly see her grab her leg when she was hit.

Through the years, I experienced my fair share of *tantruming* students. There was no common denominator. Some were boys, some were girls, some were from well-to-do families, and others lived in poverty. The one thing they all seemed to have in common was perseverance. They could scream and kick and knock things off of desks and tables for the longest time. I'd had restraint training in three districts but would only restrain a student to prevent him or her from hurting themselves or others.

Trust me, in the midst of a child's lengthy temper tantrum, you'll try about anything. You just want it to stop. It's so loud and it's discouraging—to say the least—to see all of your paperwork and books all over the floor and furniture toppled.

I remember calling my supervisor one afternoon after a student's lengthy tantrum, telling him I needed to go home to shower and change because I'd been spat upon nonstop for two hours.

No matter how loud and no matter what was being said or thrown, I always used a very quiet and calm voice. It occasionally helped the student calm down, but it always helped me to stay calm.

Sometimes it actually felt like I wasn't in the midst of the chaos but was just watching a movie. Not a pleasant movie, mind you.

A little girl's tantrum was modified quite a bit after the counselor and I convinced her that crying in the main office was against school board policy. I told her we wouldn't report it if she quieted herself because we didn't think she knew. She managed to rein in the crying and screaming.

"Yeah, I didn't know," she said, her bottom lip still quivering.

Thankfully, the little boy whose shrill screams actually hurt my ears was pretty easily convinced that the large rain stick in my office was a magic crying wand. While its hundreds of tiny metal balls spiraled their way down the see-thru acrylic tube, he could cry. I told him I'd seen it work on other students; their crying would just magically stop as soon as the rain sound stopped. He reached a point where whenever he was brought to the office, he would just head over to the corner where I kept the "magic crying wand" and would turn it over by himself and wait for it to do its thing.

A secretary I worked with would sometimes come into my office after a student had been *tantruming* for a while and say, "Mrs. Leary, do you think it's time for the calming cloth?" A few minutes later she'd appear with an ice-cold damp washcloth, which she'd gently apply to the student's forehead. Especially for younger students—a new face, a new voice, and a soothing cool cloth and a drink of water would sometimes do the trick. Then again, I once had a cup of water thrown in my face.

Sometimes little tricks worked. Sometimes nothing worked. In those instances when nothing worked, I'd sit in a chair blocking the door and just wait calmly. Wait for whatever happened first—for the parent to arrive or for the *tantruming* child to fall asleep on the floor.

I kept a pillow in the bottom drawer of my file cabinet. At some opportune time while a child was tantruming I would casually toss the pillow on the floor. Surprising how many managed to migrate toward the pillow mid-scream, cuddle up, and doze off. Tantruming is exhausting!

Once it became obvious we couldn't contain the situation, we'd put a call into the parent. That action was met with a variety of responses, from "I'm so very sorry, I'll be right there" to "So, why the hell are you calling me?"

Most parents were cooperative and well intentioned. If a parent couldn't leave work to come to the school, we always worked with them. No one wanted someone to be docked pay or even worse, lose his or her job. We would arrange to have phone conferences, provide in-school detention, etc., to accommodate parents in these situations.

One boy, whom I remember especially well, seemed to get into trouble everywhere—on the bus, in the classroom, in the cafeteria, on the playground. He was a challenge. We two had lots of long talks about his choices—about whether or not they were working for him. He could tell me the rules and tell me what he should have done instead. He could talk the talk. Walking the talk—a completely different story.

I once asked him if he ever got tired of being in trouble. He told me he didn't know what it was like to not be in trouble. Oh, my gosh! An honest and pretty revealing response.

I spoke with our counselor, psychologist, and special education teacher. We put our heads together and came up with a few ideas—experiments, really. I touched base with all of the key people in this child's school life and asked them to cut him some slack for a couple of weeks. Then, I called him into my office and told him he'd been recommended by a staff member to be on patrol because students seemed to look up to him.

"I get to go to the patrol picnic!" he said, excitedly.

There were only about three and a half weeks until the end-of-year patrol picnic, and we were all figuratively crossing our fingers and holding our breath hoping he could last that long. Staff members were trying to ignore his minor misbehaviors and, fortunately, he hadn't done anything major.

The day of the patrol picnic arrived and he boarded the bus wearing a huge smile. Driving my car, I followed the bus, just as I did every year, so I could make a quick appearance at the park where the picnic was held, and then return to school. I was walking back to my parked car when I heard an intercom announcement asking for any adult from my school to come to the security office.

And, there he was—our failed experiment—standing next to a security officer who had his large hand firmly planted on the boy's shoulder. Our student had wandered into the employee's lounge and stolen a wallet from inside a woman's purse that was hanging inside her locker.

Sometimes we win. Sometimes we lose. Who knows? Maybe those couple of weeks on patrol planted a seed. Maybe others in his life planted seeds. Maybe those seeds germinated and grew, and as he grew up he turned his life around. Then again, he might be phoning folks telling them their computer has a virus and all he needs is their Visa account number and password.

One of the boys I spent the most time with (because of behavior issues) was one who touched my heart the most. He was big and loud and had a quick temper. It didn't take much to set him off.

On the last day of school, as he was exiting the building with his class, he stepped out of line and hugged me. It surprised me and, to be honest, I expected him to let go quickly and take off with his friends. But he kept clinging to me until I could feel his shoulders begin to bounce up and down. He was crying. This fifth grader—a good five inches taller than me—was sobbing because he was leaving his elementary school. Sometimes we momentarily forget that the kids who drive us the craziest are also the ones who need us most.

As a mom was exiting the school's office I happened to notice her tee-shirt was inside out—something we asked kids to do when their shirt had inappropriate writing or pictures. Our school's secretary told me the woman explained that she'd been on her way to her ex-husband's house to pick up her child support check when we called to let her know her son was ill. When asked to do so, she graciously agreed to step into the restroom to turn the shirt inside out. "So, what did the shirt say?" I asked our secretary. Leaning forward, after looking around to make sure no students were nearby, she whispered, "Fuck you and the whore you rode in on!"

CHAPTER TWENTY-SIX

"Everybody Hurts"

THE COMPARISON OF A SCHOOL TO A TINY TOWN IS appropriate when it comes to any emergency situation. Calling 911 for an ambulance was by no means a frequent event at any school in which I worked, but we never hesitated to access their assistance and expertise when we felt it was necessary.

When a first grader got his head stuck between two vertical bars of the outdoor play structure, we tried smearing cooking oil from the school's kitchen on the bars and gently guiding his head back out. This absolutely wasn't going to work, so we placed a call to the fire department.

They had all the necessary tools and know-how needed for this kind of situation. One of the firemen saying "Bring me the saw" elicited some pretty shrill shrieks from the entrapped boy. In retrospect, I sure wish we'd foreseen this reaction and explained each step of what was happening to the little boy.

We needed to call for an ambulance when a little girl ran headfirst into a soccer goal post during recess. Her dad arrived at school in time to ride with her in the ambulance and, fortunately, she had only a knot and bruise on her forehead and a concussion.

When a fourth grader got his fingers caught underneath the cafeteria door, we were ready to call the fire department, but our quick-thinking custodian arrived with a screwdriver in hand. He loosened the door's hinges and was able to lift the door up just enough so the student could free his fingers. Nothing appeared broken, and he could move his thumb and fingers without pain, so we just had him apply ice and called the parents just to inform them.

A fifth grader was standing in the seat of the swing and jumped from it when he heard the bell ring. Somehow his foot got entangled in the chain and he pulled his leg as he was jumping. Misusing the swing for just those few seconds resulted in serious injuries to his ankle, knee, and hip. Immediately accessing 911 and his parents resulted in his quick arrival at the hospital, where he had to undergo surgery.

Sometimes, in the tiny town of a school, emergency care is also needed for the staff. A staff member was writhing in pain when the paramedics arrived. Those of us nearby were fearful she was having a heart attack. Her husband called us later that afternoon to let us know the pain was caused by kidney stones and she'd be out for a few days.

A staff assistant took a bad fall when she tripped on some ripped carpet in a classroom. The carpet was several years old and the rip had been repaired time and again with strips of duct tape, which was curling up at its edges.

We cleared the classroom of students. The ambulance arrived quickly and so did the staff assistant's husband. Head wounds tend to bleed profusely, and this one was no exception. The teacher and another staff assistant were trying to console the woman, telling her not to worry and that it wasn't as bad as she thought. She was trying so hard to keep her composure—even joking about having a scar like Harry Potter. Hitting the corner of a desktop when she fell caused a deep cut in the middle of her forehead.

I was speaking with her husband, who was understandably upset, and was asking me why the carpet was ripped and taped.

As per protocol, after calling 911 our secretary immediately called the district to explain why we called an ambulance. In the midst of this medical emergency, I got a radio call from our secretary telling me that my supervisor was on the line and wanted to speak with me. The only way for that to happen was for me to leave the situation and walk back to the office. The call couldn't be transferred. I went to a corner in the room and whispered into the radio telling the secretary to explain that everything was under control and that I'm speaking with the injured woman's very upset husband right now. I asked if I may please call back in just a few minutes. The answer was no; he wanted to talk to me now. Everyone in the room heard the response over the radio. A staff assistant looked at me, rolled his eyes, and said, "Outranked, huh?"

I hurried to the office, briefly explained on the phone what was going on, and quickly returned to the classroom. The right thing to do at the time, for both the employee and the district, would have been to stay with my injured staff member and call back later. But a school principal is a middle-management position and middle management sometimes means caught in the middle.

An office staff member was having breathing problems during the day even after using her inhaler. Despite her insistence that I not call 911, I did. She was in the midst of a serious asthma episode and the emergency medical team was recommending she be transported to the hospital. She was so angry with me, but I followed her to the hospital and was right there as they wheeled the gurney out. She smiled so widely when she saw me and I realized she wasn't angry, so much as she was scared.

During student testing, the teacher in charge was working out of my office because she needed to be where the booklets and answer sheets could be kept secure. She had just finished unpacking all of the books and had stacked their shipping boxes in a tidy tower of cardboard—one box inside the next—just inside my office's doorway.

Just a few minutes later I reentered my office, rounding the corner inside the doorway at my usual too-fast pace. Stumbling my way through the falling boxes, I fell to the floor on one knee—hard! As I fell forward, the corner of my desk was looming just inches away. I instinctively reached out with my hand to avoid running into it face first. The scans at the hospital showed torn cartilage in my left knee and the ligament stretching over my middle finger had become displaced.

I returned to work a couple of days later on crutches, with my swollen knee wrapped, and my bandaged hand suspended in a sling. Our poor reading specialist, who was serving as the school's test coordinator, probably endured more than me, having become the butt of her colleagues' endless teasing and jokes about trying to take down the principal and how she really shouldn't worry too much about how this might be reflected on her annual evaluation.

A first grader was sent to my office for saying a bad word to a girl in his class. When he arrived, he was insistent he didn't say a bad word. I asked him to repeat exactly what he said to her. The Hispanic boy, who spoke with a heavy accent, explained, "We was writing and I ask her how you make a ass?" he said, while tracing a backward letter "S" in the air with his index finger.

CHAPTER TWENTY-SEVEN

"The Great Imposter"

NOT ONLY DID THE LITTLE GIRL HAND THE CAFETERIA manager a one-hundred-dollar bill to pay for lunch, which was quite unusual, but also, there was something about the bill that just didn't look or feel quite right. A staff assistant brought the girl to the office, along with the potentially bogus Benjamin.

I looked at it and instantly knew it couldn't be real. The paper felt too thick and the margin looked too thin. I asked the little girl where she got the money, and she said she took it from underneath her uncle's bed at her house.

"I only took one," she said. "He gots lots more in his suitcase."

The staff assistant took her back to the cafeteria to get her lunch while I called the police. Two officers arrived pretty quickly and both took a look at the bill holding it up to the light. They left, saying that an agent would be notifying me to collect the bill before the day was out and, in the meantime, just put it in our safe.

Sure enough, about three hours later, two men—tall, fit, chiseled features, great hair, looking ever so James Bond-ish—arrived to retrieve the money along with the child's name and home address.

Funny how many female staff members just happened to wander into and hang around the office while the agents were there.

The ICE man cometh! Whenever we got a call that parents had been detained and were going to be deported back to their country, we knew that meant children's lives were about to be terribly disrupted. Either the parents' paperwork had expired, they didn't report for a court date, or it had been discovered that they entered the United States illegally.

Often the children were born in the United States—making them U.S. citizens. They would remain in the country—hopefully in the custody of relatives. Our instructions were to get the students from class just before the end of the day and to hold them in the office until a social services person showed up to take them. We weren't to tell the students anything. It would sure cast a heavy haze over the rest of the day. These children were in class, oblivious to what was about to happen. Their lives were going to be turned upside down indefinitely and there was absolutely nothing we could do.

I, myself, became an imposter at a very young age—in elementary school.

During lunch recess, with my best friends Lisa and Mary Anne, I tried out for our school's chorus. The problem was they could both sing and I couldn't, and I knew it. The following day the names of students who'd passed the audition were posted on a sheet of paper taped to the outside of the chorus teacher's classroom door.

Lisa and Mary Anne anxiously skimmed the alphabetical listing and, when they saw their names, started jumping up and down excitedly, squealing, "I made it! I made it! I made it!"

My name wasn't there. I didn't expect it would be. But I so wanted to be among the chosen that I pretended it was and started jumping up and down squealing right along with my two friends, "I made it! I made it! I made it!"

A couple of days later we had our first practice and a sign-in sheet was taped to a student desk just outside the classroom door. I made sure Lisa and Mary Anne signed in before me, then I picked up the pen, leaned down real close to the desktop, pretended to sign my name on the piece of paper, and followed them inside.

On that first day we learned voice warm-up exercises and sang the notes the teacher played on the piano. I was so afraid of giving away my secret that I just kept opening my mouth and pretending to sing.

Two days later it was practice day again. This time the attendance sheet had been moved inside and we were supposed to put a check mark next to our typed name. I pretended to do that, as well, quickly tracing over a check mark another student had already made. Mrs. Nason picked up the clipboard and looked at it. Then, holding her index finger up in the air she counted us.

"One, two, three, four…," she silently mouthed each number until she reached thirty-one.

During the third practice, the teacher announced that starting with the back row and going down each of the three rows, when it was our turn, she wanted us to say our name. Being shorter than most, I was standing in the front row. The voices of students calling out their names were sounding closer and closer to me. My heart pounded faster and faster. My neck and face felt hot and I was afraid I was going to cry. I thought about running out of the room, pretending I was suddenly sick. But it was my turn now so I said my name.

To my surprise and relief, the teacher smiled at me and with great flourish made a check mark on the paper attached to the clipboard she was holding. Maybe my name had been on that list, after all, and I just hadn't seen it. No, I knew that couldn't be true. So, when practice ended,

I waited to speak with the teacher privately. I was pretty sure she was going to tell me not to come back.

Practice ended. I bent down and pretended I was tying the laces on one of my black and white saddle oxfords to allow enough time for the others to leave. As the last few were exiting the door, I stepped up to her desk and said, "Mrs. Nason, my name's not on that list." She tilted her clipboard so I could see it and pointed to my name written in her teacher-perfect cursive with a big check mark right beside. Mine was the first name on the list above all of the other typed ones.

"Yes, it is," she said, smiling and giving my long ponytail a teasing tug before telling me I'd better hurry to my classroom before the bell rang.

We practiced twice a week. I never missed a practice. I loved chorus! Once in a while Mrs. Nason would remind me to quiet my voice and sing very, very softly "because it's so pretty that way."

Before we performed for the other students at the Christmas program, Mrs. Nason told me she had chosen me especially to ring a little silver bell while the others sang "Silent Night" and "Hark the Herald, Angels Sing." She said she wanted me to sing my heart out when the chorus led the whole school in singing "Jingle Bells" at the end of the program.

I was just happy Mrs. Nason wasn't mad at me and didn't kick me out of chorus. Of course, as I grew older, I realized the gifts she'd given me were far greater. She allowed me to be included in something I wanted so much and, even more, she made me feel worthy—when I wasn't. She knew I pushed my way in and yet, she warmly welcomed me into the fold. She encouraged me, praised me, and even came up with a clever way to prevent me from desecrating beautiful songs while, at the same time, allowing me to believe I was chosen for a very special job.

As a principal, I shared this personal story with the staff, at each one of my schools, and challenged them to be someone's Mrs. Nason.

When I was in my second year of teaching, our city's local newspaper did a two-page spread about the way I was teaching math. I had teamed up with Seafirst Bank. They provided checkbooks and ledgers for each of my students. I also hit up local companies for car brochures, catalogues, travel brochures, and the like, and planned a yearlong banking unit directly linked to the grade-level math standards for each quarter. Kids wrote checks for pretend purchases (like cars, groceries, and vacations), paid taxes, calculated interest, built and balanced budgets, and had daily assignments (e.g., using today's newspaper grocery ads, plan a dinner menu and make food purchases for a dinner for six people). We played a place-value game that added money to their accounts each week.

Parents were thrilled with the approach. I loved teaching actual life skills, and the kids were loving math. The article was nice recognition, but when that wasn't the end of it, I recall feeling a bit panicked but not understanding why.

"Did you see today's editorial?" a colleague asked me as we walked into the school at the same time on the morning after the math article was published.

I retrieved a copy of the newspaper from our library and almost felt lightheaded reading the headline of the double-column editorial: "If you think math is important then you'll love Karen Leary's classroom!"

This is too much, I was thinking. Way too much.

I avoided going into the staff room that day, thinking the other teachers were probably upset by the attention I was getting, and who could blame them?

These same uncomfortable feelings crept up when one morning almost every staff member I encountered congratulated me. Although it was my first year in both that district and that school, I had been voted the school's "Teacher of the Year." I knew I should feel honored, but mostly I was just surprised. It was my first year there and they didn't even really know me. The others who'd been there so much longer were probably upset with me.

When I moved to the next level of the competition and was named regional "Teacher of the Year," I felt uncomfortable. It's difficult to explain the feeling. It's different than feeling humbled; it's more like feeling unworthy.

As a first-year administrator in another district, I was asked to accompany the superintendent to a national conference in San Francisco to do a presentation. One of our technology gurus accompanied him, as well. I wrote the script for the presentation and the tech expert captured each page to match my presentation so it would appear as though we were actually tapping into our website live, but there'd be no slow start-up, no lost connections, no glitches. The superintendent introduced me to the crowd, and I spoke for forty minutes about our student information system.

My husband and the superintendent's wife flew to San Francisco that evening to join us. An educational curriculum company treated us to an elaborate happy hour at the hotel followed by a multicourse dinner at one of San Francisco's premier restaurants.

Why am I here? I was thinking, feeling a little like I did when I'd sneaked my way into chorus.

The following year, George W. Bush was hitting the presidential campaign trail and chose to unveil his "No Child Left Behind" platform during a news conference in the district where I worked. The superintendent said he wanted me to be on the panel during the news conference. I incorrectly assumed it must be a big panel.

On the day of the news conference, I was excited and felt fairly comfortable because there were plenty of friendly faces in the audience. But then, when extremely bright television camera lights were turned on and I could no longer see anyone in the audience, I felt my heart beat quicken. I looked down at the row of people seated behind the skirted table—the school board president, the superintendent, the presidential candidate, and me.

I felt kind of like the ordinary person behind the curtain in "The Wizard of Oz." At any moment someone might rip away the gossamer fabric that was hiding who I really was. Or, worse yet, someone might take attendance and my name would not be on the list. Why should I be here? I'm an associate principal. Everyone is more senior than me.

I just recently learned there is a name for this feeling: *Imposter Syndrome*. Imposter syndrome (also called Perceived Fraudulence) involves feelings of self-doubt that persist despite one's education, experience, and accomplishments. It's apparently not uncommon.

I remember there were so many times I'd drive onto the campus of a school I'd been assigned to and I'd be proudly and thankfully thinking—Wow! I'm in charge of this whole school. But, I'll confess, there were also times when I'd drive onto the campus and I'd be nearly panic-stricken thinking—Oh my God, I can't believe I'm in charge of this whole school.

Sometimes I felt accomplished and confident. Other times, for whatever reason, I felt like that little girl who couldn't spell if her life depended on it, who dropped the chalk during arithmetic races to hide that she didn't understand multiplication, who sneaked her way into chorus, and now—somehow—she's the principal of a school.

I kind of think maybe none of us really knows what we're doing one-hundred percent of the time and we're all just pretending we do.

Years ago, I watched the comedy movie *"Funny Farm,"* starring Chevy Chase. In the movie, the idyllic farm and small town that a couple decided to move to had both proven to be anything but idyllic. Chevy Chase pays the townsfolk to "act normal," so he and his now-estranged wife can have a hope of selling their farm. He provides them Norman Rockwell's *"Saturday Evening Post"* covers to show what normal looks like. At one point, when potential buyers are looking out the window, Chevy Chase says, via a walkie-talkie, "Cue the deer," and a townsperson releases a deer who then gracefully leaps across the meadow.

"Cue the deer" became one school's warning every time we needed to get ready for a visiting VIP—even when the VIP was from within our own district.

We would "cue the deer!" when a school board member, or the superintendent, or someone from outside the district was making a visit to our school. We did this to keep from revealing the challenges we faced or exposing visitors to student misbehaviors. For the duration of anyone's visit we were essentially imposters.

One of the most fraudulent displays was when a top district office person wanted to bring a photographer to our school. He was receiving an award he'd applied for and these photos might be included in an article about him. His administrative assistant called and told me the exact day and time he and the photographer would be on campus and said we were to highlight students using technology. I explained that the time he proposed was lunch time. Kids would either be at recess or in the cafeteria. No one would be in the classrooms.

"Well, can't you just change the schedule?" he asked.

Okay, I changed the schedule. I also chose one of the smoothest running classrooms and asked the teacher to discard whatever she had planned and, instead, have students working on their tablets, per request. I pulled three students who had behavioral issues and housed them in other classrooms during the photo shoot and inserted a staff assistant to help out. "Cue the deer."

I certainly wasn't the only principal doing this. There was a strongly inferred expectation that everything would look as perfect as possible. If I had it all to do over again, I wouldn't "cue the deer." It's good for others to experience the path educators walk on a daily basis—with all of its steep inclines and ruts and bumps included. Staging the "perfect" tour, adding support staff, and excluding misbehaving students were false representations of reality.

One time, "cueing the deer" wasn't possible due to a tight timeline, and it ended up being completely unnecessary, anyway. For this particular group, any school would have looked perfect even on the most challenging of days.

About an hour before school let out, I received a call from the district letting me know that a group of educators from Africa had been visiting the district and wanted to see a school. I asked when we might expect them.

"Look out the window," she answered.

Sure enough, a small group of men were walking toward the entry. There was no time to prepare anyone or stage anything. After hurrying to the front of the building, I warmly welcomed the gentlemen and took them on a tour. They were so gracious and in awe of everything. "The building is so big!" "There is so much space!" "The children have desks!" "They do not share books!"

I asked the visiting teacher walking nearest me what his classroom was like. He smiled.

"We do not have rooms," he said. "We teach outside."

"I have been teaching the longest," he said, beaming with pride, "I teach beneath the biggest tree."

It's good to see ourselves through the eyes of others. So often, it awakens a more grateful and appreciative spirit in us.

When my husband and I were nearing retirement, we decided we would assemble and hang a paper clip chain in each of our offices. These chains served as a visual reminders of the exact amount of time we had left before retirement—one paper clip represented one month. As a discreet celebratory countdown, on the last day of each month we'd remove a paper clip and toss it into the trash at the end of the day.

At first, the linked chain seemed as if it was taking forever to become shorter. Then, one day the tinny sound of the paper clip hitting the side of the metal trash can marked the halfway point.

After that, the last clips seemed to come off quickly, and I became keenly aware that each clip marked not only the end of a month but also "the last" of so many things that had been a part of my life for decades. It was the last first day of school, the last book fair, the last Christmas program, the last promotion ceremony, and even the last Tuesday meeting.

Like the last bite of a rich dessert, at the end of a multicourse dinner, these "lasts" were savored. Much like everything appears smaller in a rearview mirror, everything coming to an end seems a bit sweeter. I made a conscious decision to watch the faces of the children during performances instead of watching the doors and parking lot for potential problems. I spoke to students about their choices at the book fair instead of being on the lookout for shoplifting. I felt free to focus on the children's eyes and smiles instead of on their data.

Those last few months reminded me of why I became a teacher in the first place. As a teacher, I did my best to plan and present instruction in a way so that my students would enjoy learning. Because they enjoyed learning, they learned. Student success was never the goal of my instruction; it was the byproduct of my instruction.

One chilly Wednesday afternoon in January, I stood in front of the staff of what would become the last school of my career.

"At this very moment, my husband is across town telling his staff he's retiring at the end of this school year," I said, "and, I'm here telling you that I will be doing the very same thing."

It was a surprise to me how emotional I felt hearing myself say those words out loud. I didn't expect my voice would crack.

A couple of people, who were themselves contemplating retirement, asked me how I decided to retire. Did I just instinctively know it was time?

"Oh, hell yeah!"

My mind and heart were still willing and able but, my body was in a completely different time zone. I moved a little slower, it was a little harder to hear those tiny kindergarten voices. What can I say? I no longer peed like a horse.

I knew, in retirement, I'd miss my colleagues and, of course, I'd miss the kids. But, I was pretty sure I wouldn't miss that 5:45 A.M. alarm, nor only being able to travel during spring and winter breaks, nor the echoing noise in a cafeteria, nor standing crosswalk duty in the pouring rain.

I'll also confess to having grown weary of too many annual unveilings of new programs, new curricula, new expectations, new data, new assessments, new technology—all aimed at raising test scores—like some victorious secret. Maybe, the secret is, there is no secret—other than having a skilled and caring teacher in every classroom. High test scores are not the goal of masterful teaching—they are the byproduct.

Once my decision was made, regarding when I would retire, I looked forward to it. I felt proud of my accomplishments and very grateful for my opportunities and experiences. When the time came, we celebrated in style. After my husband and I flew the coop, we flew to Italy, with our children and grandchildren.

These days we sleep in late, stay up late, and have "happy hour" dinners. My husband plays music and I write. There is a lot to be said for freedom. For the first time in my life, I am the boss of me!

My childhood dream came to fruition. I was that little at-risk girl who, thanks to teachers, became a teacher. Stepping into the role of principal (in red high heels, of course), I was blessed to spend my days in the company of children and educators—and, let me tell you, it doesn't get much better than that.

When I reflect upon my years as a principal, I'll confess, there were some scary times and some sad times, but many, many days were filled with joy and laughter. Through the years, whenever something funny or tragic or silly or frightening happened at one of my schools, invariably, someone would say to me, "You know, you really should write a book."

And, so—I did.

Final Confession…

Remember that "Out of Order" sign that was periodically taped to the laminating machine? In each school, the laminating machine was only <u>sometimes</u> out of order. I do hope you all forgive me—because that little sign sure did help us stretch our schools' budgets so we could stay in the black until the end of the school year.